1500
CALIFORNIA
Place Names

Their Origin and Meaning

A revised version of *1000 California Place Names*,
by Erwin G. Gudde, third edition

William Bright

❦

UNIVERSITY OF CALIFORNIA PRESS
Berkeley   Los Angeles   London

University of California Press
Berkeley and Los Angeles, California

University of California Press, Ltd.
London, England

© 1998 by The Regents of the University of California

Library of Congress Cataloging-in-Publication Data

Bright, William, 1928–
    1500 California place names : their origin and
    meaning / William Bright.
        p.   cm.
    "A revised version of 1000 California place names,
by Erwin G. Gudde, third edition."
    ISBN 0-520-21271-1 (alk. paper)
    1. Names, Geographical—California.
2. California—History, Local.   I. Gudde, Erwin
Gustav, 1889–1969.   1000 California place names
II. Title.   III. Title: 1500 California place names.
IV. Title: Fifteen hundred California place names.
F859. G8   1998
917.94'001' 4—dc21   97-43147

Printed in the United States of America
11 10 09 08 07 06 05 04
12 11 10 9 8 7 6 5 4

1500
California Place Names

The Counties of
Present-Day California

Preface

THIS BOOK IS the descendant of several others. In 1947, the University of California Press published a small book called *1000 California Place Names,* by Professor Erwin G. Gudde, of the University of California at Berkeley. In 1949, the Press published a larger volume, reporting in full on Gudde's place-name research up to that time; the title of that work was *California Place Names: The Origin and Etymology of Current Geographical Names.* The success of both those books warranted updated versions in the following years: second and third editions of the "small book" were published in 1949 and 1971, while a second edition of the "big book" appeared in 1960, and a third in 1969—the year of Gudde's death. Most recently, I have myself carried out a new updating of Gudde's "big book," which will appear as a revised fourth edition in 1998, with Gudde named as author and myself as editor.

A special effort was made in this new edition not only to incorporate fresh data on California place names in general, but also to give more reliable information on names of Native American origin, based on recent field research by linguists and anthropologists working with living speakers of California Indian languages.

In preparing a new "small book," the present *1500 California Place Names*, I wanted to produce a book on California place-name origins that, like Gudde's *1000 California Place Names*, would be attractive to Californians and convenient to use. For this reason, the book is restricted to two classes of names: first, those that are "famous" because they refer to well-known geographical features of the state, like San Diego, Tahoe, and Yreka; and second, those that may refer to lesser-known locations but are "of interest" because of their problematic origins, especially when they derive from Spanish—names like Arrastre, Bodega, and Chamisal—or from American Indian languages—names like Chirpchatter, Loleta, and Cuyamaca. (A few names have gone through both Indian and Spanish versions; in Santa Barbara County, the Chumash name *kalawashaq,* meaning "turtle shell," was reinterpreted as Spanish *calabazal,* "pumpkin patch," before entering English as the name of Calabazal Creek.) For the large number of names that fall "in the middle"—places like Johnsondale and Johnstonville and Johnsville—readers are directed to the fourth edition of the "big book," *California Place Names*.

In addition to place names, this book also includes names of the major Indian tribes of California. Some of these have themselves been adapted as place names, and others are referred to as the sources of place names.

I should make it clear that *1500 California Place Names* is not simply an expansion of the earlier "small book"; rather, it is a new work, based on the information that I gathered for the larger work. Of course I am indebted, above all, to the earlier work by Gudde; but in addition I must express my gratitude to the many people who provided new information when I was carrying out that revision. One group consists of several dozen local historians, authors, government employees, teachers, librarians, and knowledgeable California residents; I have thanked them by name in the larger volume. A second group consists of my fellow specialists in California Indian languages, and I wish to repeat my thanks to the following scholars in particular: Catherine Callaghan, Catherine Fowler, Victor Golla, Margaret Langdon, John McLaughlin, Pamela Munro, Robert Oswalt, Alice Shepherd, and William Shipley. Responsibility for all use of published or unpublished material is, of course, mine alone.

I have tried to provide information on the local pronunciations of place names, employing a system of phonetic transcription familiar from most English dictionaries. However, it is often difficult to fix upon a single "correct" pronunciation. In California and the Southwest, this problem arises especially with regard to names of Spanish origin. The word *cañada,* "valley," is pronounced in Spanish approximately as *kahn YAH dhah,* but such an utterance is rarely heard among Californians who are speaking English. What one hears, of course, is a range of pronunciations, including *kuhn YAH duh, kuhn YAD uh, kuh NAH duh,* and *KAN uh duh;* and all these must be recognized. None are incorrect, but they are used by people with different social backgrounds and attitudes—conservative or innovative, Anglo oriented or Hispano oriented. By contrast, a conceivable pronunciation like *kuh NAY duh* simply does not occur among local residents; it could be used only by the greenest newcomer.

With regard to Native American origins of place names, it has to be acknowledged that some are not fully understood and are likely to remain forever obscure—especially in the long-missionized southern and central areas of California. Many of the original languages are no longer spoken, and the cultures have dwindled. But the California Indian people are still our neighbors, and we live on sites that were founded by their ancestors. The names that those ancestors gave to California places are still on our tongues.

William Bright
Boulder, Colorado
August 1997

Key to Pronunciation

THE PRONUNCIATION of many California place names is obvious from their spelling. In other cases, however, this book indicates pronunciations phonetically within parentheses. Note the values of the following symbols:

a	as in	*cap, bad, act*
ah		*far, father, spa, cot, fond*
air		*air, fare, there*
aw		*law, dawn, caught* (many people pronounce this the same as the *o* [ah] in *cot*)
ay		*day, wait, cape*
ch		*child, church*
dh		like *th* in *then, bathe, rather*
e		*set, red, left*
ee		*tree, east, eve*
er		*her, sir, fur, upper*

g	as in	*go, give, gag*
i		*it, bid, ink*
ie		*die, my, high;* before a consonant, written *i . . . e,* as in *side, bite, line*
ng		*sing, long*
oh		*oh, oak, own, vote*
oo		*boot, soon, coop*
or		*or, soar, tore*
ow		*cow, down, out*
oy		*boy, coin, soil*
s		*sun, case, miss* (not the *z* sound in *rose, boys*)
sh		*crash*
th		*thin, thick, think* (not the sound of *then, bathe,* which is written here as *dh*)
u		*put, book, look*
uh		*but, sun, rug;* also the unaccented vowel of *sofa, alone*
zh		*measure, azure*

The following phonetic symbols occur in languages other than English:

'	represents a glottal stop, i.e., an interruption of the breath in the throat, as in *oh-oh!* or in a careful pronunciation of *the* (') *ice*
č	like *ch* in *church*
ə	the unaccented *a* of *sofa, appear, alone*
ï	like *oo* in *boot,* but with the lips flat instead of rounded
ł	like English *l,* but without vibration of the vocal cords; the same as Welsh *ll*

ñ	like *ny* in *canyon*
š	like *sh* in *ship*
ṣ	like *s* with the tip of the tongue pulled back
ṭ	like *t* with the tip of the tongue pulled back (somewhat as in *heart*)

The syllable that carries the principal accent is capitalized; for example, the pronunciation of the word *Mono* is shown as *MOH noh*.

1500
California Place Names

❦

ABALONE (ab uh LOH nee) **POINT** [Humboldt Co.]. The abalone, an edible shellfish, has given its name to several places in California. The term comes from Rumsen (Costanoan), in which *awlun* means "red abalone."

ACALANES (ah kuh LAH neez) [Contra Costa Co.]. Refers to a Indian tribe of the Miwokan family, living south of San Pablo and Suisun Bays, whom the Spanish called Sacalanes. The term *Los Sacalanes* was reinterpreted as *Los Acalanes* in the 1830s. The tribe is now usually referred to as Saklan.

ACHUMAWI (ah choo MAH wee). An American Indian group of Shasta, Lassen, and Modoc Counties; also called the Pit River tribe. Their language is related to the neighboring Atsugewi. The alternative spelling Ahjumawi occurs in the name of **Ahjumawi Lava Springs State Park** [Shasta Co.].

ACRODECTES (ak roh DEK teez) **PEAK** [Kings Canyon N.P.]. Although the word resembles an Ancient Greek name, it does not exist in the ancient language; it is a zoological name, coined from Greek *akros*, "peak," and *dektēs*, "biter," to refer to *Acrodectes philopagus*, a rare species of cricket found only in the high Sierra.

ADELANTO (ad uh LAN toh) [San Bernardino Co.]. A name given in recent times; the Spanish word means "progress" or "advance."

ADOBE (uh DOH bee) **CREEK** [Mendocino Co.]. The Spanish term *adobe*, found in many place names, refers to a claylike soil suitable for making bricks, to such bricks themselves, or to a building constructed from adobe bricks.

AGASSIZ (AG uh see), **MOUNT** [Kings Canyon N.P.]. Named for Louis Agassiz, a Swiss-American scientist of the nineteenth century.

AGNEW [Santa Clara Co.]. Named for Abram Agnew and his family, who settled in the Santa Clara Valley in 1873. The name was later applied to a state mental hospital at the site.

AGOURA (uh GOO ruh) [Los Angeles Co.]. Named for Pierre Agoure, a Basque who had a ranch here in the 1890s.

AGUA (AH gwuh). From the Spanish for "water"; the word occurs in many combinations to form place names, such as **Agua Caliente** (kal ee EN tee) [Sonoma Co.], "hot water" (i.e., hot springs); **Agua Fria** (FREE uh) [Mariposa Co.], "cold water"; **Agua Dulce** (DOOL see) [Los Angeles Co.], "sweet water"; and **Agua Hedionda** (hed ee AHN duh) [San Diego Co.], "stinking water" (probably referring to sulfur springs).

AGUANGA (uh WAHNG guh) [Riverside Co.]. From a Luiseño village name, *awáanga,* "dog place," from *awáal,* "dog."

AGUEREBERRY (AG er bair ee) **POINT** [Death Valley N.P.]. Named, using an alternative spelling, for "French Pete" Aguerreberry, a Basque miner who worked here around 1906.

AHA KWIN (uh hah KWIN) **PARK** [Riverside Co.]. From Mojave *'ahá,* "water," and *aakwín-,* "to bend."

AHJUMAWI (ah joo MAH wee) **LAVA SPRINGS STATE PARK** [Shasta Co.]. Named for the Indian group (also spelled Achumawi), locally called the Pit River tribe, who are native to the area. Their name in their language, *ajumaawi,* "river people," from *ajuma,* "river," originally referred to the Fall River band of this tribe.

AHWAHNEE (uh WAH nee) [Yosemite N.P.]. From Southern Sierra Miwok *awooni,* "Yosemite Valley," from *awwo,* "mouth."

AHWIYAH (uh WIE yuh) **POINT** [Yosemite N.P.]. From Southern Sierra Miwok *awaaya,* "lake" or "deep." Mirror Lake was earlier called Ahwiyah Lake.

ALABAMA HILLS [Inyo Co.]. The term was applied by Southern sympathizers in 1863, after the Confederate raider *Alabama* sank the Union warship *Hatteras* off the coast of Texas.

ALAMAR (al uh MAHR) **CANYON** [Santa Barbara Co.]. From the Spanish for "place of poplar (or cottonwood) trees," from *álamo,* "poplar (or cottonwood)."

ALAMBIQUE (al uhm BEEK) **CREEK** [San Mateo Co.]. From the Spanish for "still," a place where liquor is distilled. Moonshiners, it seems, once worked in the area.

ALAMEDA (al uh MEE duh). Spanish for "grove of poplar (or cottonwood) trees," from *álamo*, "poplar (or cottonwood)," or for a grove of shade trees in general. The term dates from 1794; it was applied to the city and to **Alameda County** in 1853.

ALAMILLA (ah luh MEE yuh) **SPRING** [Amador Co.]. Not from *álamo*. Rather, it was named by José María Amador in 1826, when he built his adobe house about a mile—*a la milla,* "at the mile"—west of the spring.

ALAMITOS (al uh MEE tuhs) **BAY** [Los Angeles Co.]. From the Spanish for "little poplars (or cottonwoods)," the diminutive of *álamo*.

ALAMO (AL uh moh) [Contra Costa Co.]. The town takes its name from Spanish *álamo,* "poplar (or cottonwood)." The **Alamo River** [Imperial Co.] is one of the many places in the desert regions named for the Fremont cottonwood (*Populus fremontii*), which promised water to the thirsty wanderer. **Alamorio** (al uh muh REE oh) [Imperial Co.] is on the Alamo River; the name is coined from *álamo* plus Spanish *río,* "river." The plural form, *álamos,* occurs in the name of **Los Alamos** [Santa Barbara Co.].

ALBANY [Alameda Co.]. Named after the New York State birthplace of Frank J. Roberts, the town's first mayor.

ALBERHILL (al ber HIL) [Riverside Co.]. Coined from the surnames of C. H. Albers and James and George Hill, owners of the land on which the town was built about 1890.

ALBION (AL bee uhn) [Mendocino Co.]. In 1579, Sir Francis Drake landed on the northern California coast and called it New Albion. This ancient name for Britain, from Latin *albus,* "white," originally referred to the white cliffs of Dover. The term was applied to the Mendocino location in 1844.

ALCATRAZ (AL kuh traz) [San Francisco Co.]. From the Spanish for "pelican." The island has been famous first as a federal prison, then as a site of American Indian activism, and now as a museum.

ALESSANDRO (al uh ZAN droh) [Riverside Co.]. Named in 1887 after the Indian hero in Helen Hunt Jackson's romantic novel *Ramona.* Jackson perhaps confused *Alessandro,* the Italian equivalent of *Alexander,* with the Spanish *Alejandro.*

ALGODONES (al guh DOH nuhs) [Imperial Co.]. Derived from the name of a Yuman tribe that once lived on both sides of the Colorado River; they were called *halchidóom* by the neighboring Mojave tribe. (The term is not from Spanish *algodón,* "cotton.")

ALHAMBRA (al HAM bruh) [Los Angeles Co.]. Laid out in 1874 and named for the Moorish palace in Granada, Spain, made popular by Washington Irving's book *The Alhambra.* But **Alhambra Valley** [Contra Costa Co.] is a "prettying up" of Spanish Cañada del Hambre, "valley of hunger."

ALISAL (AL uh sal) [Monterey Co.]. From the Spanish for "alder grove," from *aliso,* "alder" (also sometimes applied to the sycamore). **El Alisal,** the Los Angeles home of the writer Charles Lummis, is now a museum.

ALISO (uh LEE soh) **CREEK** [Orange Co.]. From the Spanish for "alder (or sycamore)."

ALLEGHANY (AL uh gay nee) [Sierra Co.]. Named after the Alleghany Mine of the 1850s. The name goes back to the Delaware (Algonquian) name for the Allegheny River of Pennsylvania, perhaps meaning "beautiful stream."

ALMADEN (al muh DEN) [Santa Clara Co.]. The site of a cinnabar mine, from which mercury was produced; it was named in 1846 after Almadén in Spain, the world's largest such mine. California Indians used the cinnabar ore for body paint.

ALMANOR (AL muh nawr) **LAKE** [Plumas Co.]. Named after *Ali*ce, *Ma*rtha, and Eli*nore*, the daughters of Guy C. Earl, president of the power company that created this reservoir in 1917.

ALPINE [San Diego Co.]. The name was suggested in the 1880s by an early resident who said the district resembled her native Switzerland. **Alpine County,** also named for its mountainous terrain, was created in 1864 from parts of five adjacent counties; it had previously been considered part of Nevada. It now has the smallest population of any California county.

ALTA. The Spanish adjective meaning "high" or "upper" has always been a favorite in California place-naming, as in *Alta California,* "upper California," the term that the Spanish used in distinction to *Baja California.* But many names were applied in American times, such as **Altaville** [Calaveras Co.]; **Altamont** [Alameda Co.], scene of a notorious Rolling Stones concert in 1969; and **Alta Loma** [San Bernardino Co.], meaning "high hill." **Altadena** (al tuh DEE nuh) [Los Angeles Co.] was coined in 1886 from *alta* plus the last part of *Pasadena,* because of the town's situation above Pasadena.

AL TAHOE [El Dorado Co.]. From the Al Tahoe Hotel, built in 1907 by Almerin R. Sprague and named for himself—Al(merin's) Tahoe hotel.

ALTURAS (al TOOR uhs) [Modoc Co.]. Formerly called Dorrisville, the town was renamed in 1876 from the Spanish word meaning "heights," from *alto,* "high."

ALVARADO (al vuh RAH doh) [Alameda Co.]. Named in 1853 in honor of Juan Bautista Alvarado, governor of California from 1836 to 1842. A major street in Los Angeles also bears his name.

ALVISO (al VEE soh) [Santa Clara Co.]. Named in 1849 for Ignacio Alviso, who had come to the area from Mexico with the Anza expedition in 1776.

AMADOR (AM uh dohr) **COUNTY**. Named in 1854 for José María Amador, who came to California as a soldier in the Spanish garrison of San Francisco and became a big landowner. **Amador City** was founded in 1863 and named after the county.

AMARGOSA (am er GOH suh) **RIVER** [Death Valley N.P.]. From Spanish *amargoso,* "bitter" (an alternate form of *amargo*); the name was recorded by Frémont in 1844 and probably refers to alkaline water.

AMAYA (uh MAH yuh) **CREEK** [Santa Cruz Co.]. On land owned around 1860 by two Californio brothers, Casimero and Darío Amaya.

AMBOY [San Bernardino Co.]. Named as one of a series of railroad stations in alphabetical order: Amboy, Bristol, Cadiz, Danby, Edson, Fenner, and Goffs. All these names were probably taken from locations "back east."

AMERICAN RIVER [Placer, El Dorado, Sacramento Cos.]. The name was given by Sutter in the 1840s, because a ford in the river was called El Paso de los Americanos, "the crossing of the Americans," by Spanish-speaking Indians, referring to Canadian trappers.

ANACAPA (an uh KAP uh) **ISLANDS** [Ventura Co.]. The term is from Chumash *anyapax,* "mirage, illusion," recorded in 1792 by George Vancouver as both Eneeapah and Enecapa.

ANAHEIM (AN uh hime) [Orange Co.]. Named by German settlers after the Santa Ana River plus German *Heim,* "home."

ANAHUAC (AH nuh wahk) **SPRING** [San Diego Co.]. From the Diegueño place name Iñaja, but confused with Anahuac (ah NAH wahk), a name that the Aztecs gave to their Mexican homeland.

ANGELES (AN juh luhs) **NATIONAL FOREST** [Los Angeles, San Bernardino Cos.]. So named in 1908, because the larger part of the forest is within Los Angeles County.

ANGEL ISLAND [San Francisco Bay]. A translation of Spanish Isla de los Ángeles, the name given in 1775.

ANGELS CAMP [Calaveras Co.]. Named during the Gold Rush for a miner named George or Henry Angel.

AÑO NUEVO (AN oh noo AY voh, AN yoh NWAY voh) **POINT** [San Mateo Co.]. From the Spanish for "new year," so named by Vizcaíno on January 3, 1603, because it was the first promontory sighted in the new year.

ANTELOPE VALLEY [Los Angeles Co.]. Named not for a true antelope, but for the pronghorn, which was once abundant in the state.

ANTIOCH (AN tee ahk) [Contra Costa Co.]. From a city in Syria, mentioned in the Bible; the name was selected by residents at a Fourth of July picnic in 1851.

ANZA-BORREGO DESERT STATE PARK [San Diego Co.]. Formerly called Anza Desert State Park, it was named for the explorer Juan Bautista de Anza, who crossed the area in 1774. It incorporates the Borrego Desert (from a Spanish word for "sheep").

APTOS (AP tohs, AHP tohs) [Santa Cruz Co.]. A Spanish rendering, dating from 1791, of a Costanoan Indian village name, *aptoṣ,* of unknown meaning.

ARBUCKLE [Colusa Co.]. Named in 1875 for the rancher T. R. Arbuckle, who had settled here in 1866.

ARCADIA [Los Angeles Co.]. Named around 1888 for a district in ancient Greece that was considered an ideal of rural simplicity.

ARCATA (ahr KAY tuh) [Humboldt Co.]. The town is in the territory of the Wiyot Indians, but its name is from the language of a neighboring tribe: Yurok *oket'oh,* "where there is a lagoon"—referring to Humboldt Bay.

ARENA (uh REE nuh), **POINT** [Mendocino Co.]. From Spanish *arena,* "sand"; named Barro de Arena, "sand bar," by the British navigator George Vancouver in 1792.

ARGUELLO (ahr GWEL oh), **POINT** [Santa Barbara Co.]. Named in 1792 by George Vancouver after José Darío Argüello, then the Spanish commander at Monterey.

ARGUS RANGE [Inyo Co.]. The mining district was named for a giant in Greek mythology who had a hundred eyes.

AROMAS (uh ROH muhs) [Monterey Co.]. Spanish for "odors, aromas," probably referring to hot sulfur springs.

ARRASTRE (uh RAS truh) **CREEK** [San Bernardino Co.]. In Mexican Spanish, the term refers to an apparatus used for crushing ore in gold-mining days. It occurs as a place name in several areas, sometimes spelled Arrastra or Arastra.

ARROWHEAD SPRINGS and **LAKE** [San Bernardino Co.]. Named in 1860 because of an arrowhead-shaped configuration in the earth near the springs.

ARROYO (uh ROY oh). The Spanish word for "creek, watercourse" forms part of many place names. Familiar combinations include **Arroyo Seco** (SAY koh) [Los Angeles Co.], "dry creek"; and **Arroyo Grande** (GRAN dee) [San Luis Obispo Co.], "big creek."

ARROZ (uh ROHZ) [Yolo Co.]. Spanish for "rice," a major crop of the area. A town in Glenn County is called **Riz,** the French equivalent.

ARTESIA (ahr TEE zhuh) [Los Angeles Co.]. Named for artesian wells dug here in the 1870s. Artesia is the Latin name for the town of Artois in France, where artesian wells occur.

ARTOIS (AHR toys) [Glenn Co.]. Previously called Germantown, it was renamed Artois during World War I, after the French city, which was the scene of fighting.

ASILOMAR (uh SIL oh mahr, uh SEE loh mahr) [Monterey Co.]. The artificial name, coined from Spanish *asilo,* "asylum, refuge," plus *mar,* "sea," was given by the YWCA to the site in 1913.

ASTI (AS tee) [Sonoma Co.]. Named in 1881 after the city in Italy, a wine-producing center.

ASUNCION (uh SUHN see uhn) [San Luis Obispo Co.]. The Spanish word *Asunción* refers to the Assumption of the Virgin Mary—her bodily transportation to heaven. The name was given in 1776. It has sometimes been confused with the Ascension (*Ascensión* in Spanish), which refers not to Mary but to Christ.

ATASCADERO (uh tas kuh DAIR oh) [San Luis Obispo Co.]. Spanish for "a place where one gets stuck in the mud," from *atascar,* "to mire down"; the name has been used since the 1870s.

ATHERTON [San Mateo Co.]. Named in the 1860s for Faxon D. Atherton, on whose land the town was built. He was the father-in-law of the California novelist Gertrude Atherton.

ATSUGEWI (aht soo GAY wee). The name of an Indian group, also called the Hat Creek tribe, in Shasta and Lassen Counties; their language is related to Achumawi.

AUBURN [Placer Co.]. Named in 1849 by miners from Auburn, New York—which in turn was named for Auburn in England, the "loveliest village of the plain," made famous by Oliver Goldsmith's poem "The Deserted Village."

AVALON (AV uh lahn) [Los Angeles Co.]. This town on Santa Catalina Island was named in 1887 for an island in the King Arthur legend, represented as an earthly paradise of the western seas.

AVAWATZ (AV uh wahts) **MOUNTAINS** [San Bernardino Co.]. From Southern Paiute *ávawats,* "gypsum."

AVENAL (AV uh nuhl) [Kings Co.]. From the Spanish for "oat field," because of wild oats growing in the area; from *avena,* "oats." The name of **Avenal Creek** is recorded from 1891, and the town was named in 1929.

AVI COROTATH (uh VEE kohr uh TAHTH) [San Bernardino Co.]. From Mojave *'avíi,* "rock, mountain," and *kwalatáth-,* "to be big and round." It is also called Monument Peak.

AVILA (uh VIL uh, AV uh luh) [San Luis Obispo Co.]. Named for Miguel Ávila, a Spanish soldier who took up land here in 1839.

AVISADERO (uh vee zuh DAIR oh), **POINT** [San Francisco Co.]. The name for the tip of Hunters Point is from the Spanish for "place of advising or warning," from *avisar,* "to warn."

AZUSA (uh ZOO suh) [Los Angeles Co.]. Represents the name of a Gabrielino Indian village, *ashúkshanga,* of unknown meaning. Local folklore claims that the town was named because a general store (of later years) sold everything "from A to Z in the U.S.A."

BADEN-POWELL (BAY duhn POH uhl), **MOUNT** [Los Angeles Co.]. Named for Sir Robert S. S. Baden-Powell, founder of the Boy Scouts.

BAKER [San Bernardino Co.]. Named in 1908 for R. C. Baker, president of the Tonopah and Tidewater Railroad.

BAKERSFIELD [Kern Co.]. Named in 1868 for a parcel of land, "Baker's field," belonging to Colonel Thomas Baker, a civil and hydraulic engineer.

BALBOA (bal BOH uh) [Orange Co.]. Named in 1905 for Vasco Núñez de Balboa, the first European to come upon the Pacific Ocean.

BALDWIN PARK [Los Angeles Co.]. Once the property of E. J. "Lucky" Baldwin, a financier who got his nickname after he bought silver-mine stock at two dollars a share, then sold it in 1872 for eighteen hundred dollars a share. In his latter years he was embroiled in sensational lawsuits, both marital and extramarital. **Baldwin Lake** [San Bernardino Co.] was also named for him.

BALDY. The term is often applied to bare peaks, such as **Old Baldy** [San Bernardino Co.], also called **San Antonio Peak;** the nearby community of **Mount Baldy** shares the name.

BALLENA (buh LEE nuh, buh YAY nuh) **VALLEY** [San Diego Co.]. Applied in 1821, the name contains the Spanish word for "whale," referring to the shape of a nearby hill.

BALLONA (buh LOH nuh) **CREEK** [Los Angeles Co.]. From the Ballona land grant of 1839; probably a misspelling of Bayona, the name of a town in Spain.

BALLY; BOLLY; BULLY. All three forms are derived from Wintu *buli,* "mountain," and form part of the names of several mountains in northern California. The English pronunciations *BAL ee, BAH lee,* and *BUL ee* all occur. In Wintu, Bully Choop means "mountain peak"; Winnibulli is "middle mountain," and Yolla Bolly is "snow mountain."

BANNING [Riverside Co.]. Named in 1885 for Phineas Banning, a pioneer developer in southern California; he operated the first stagecoach line between Los Angeles and San Pedro.

BARONA (buh ROH nuh) **INDIAN RESERVATION** [San Diego Co.]. Named in 1846 for Father Barona, a priest at San Diego Mission.

BARRANCA (buh RANG kuh). This Spanish word for "ravine, gulch" has entered English in California names such as **Barranca Colorada** (kahl uh RAD uh) [Tehama Co.], meaning "red ravine."

BARSTOW [San Bernardino Co.]. Originally called Fishpond, in 1886 it was renamed by the Santa Fe Railroad for its president, William Barstow Strong.

BATEQUITOS (bah tuh KEE tohs) **LAGOON** [San Diego Co.]. The Spanish name, meaning "little water holes," was applied by Padre Pedro Font in 1776. It is the plural diminutive form of *batequi,* a word used in northwestern Mexico to mean "a hole dug in a dry streambed in order to find water." The origin is Yaqui *bate'ekim.*

BEALVILLE [Kern Co.]. Named for General Edward F. Beale, who served in the 1860s as U.S. surveyor general of California; however, Abraham Lincoln complained that Beale made himself "monarch of all he surveyed."

BEAR. The name of this animal occurs in hundreds of California place names, referring either to the grizzly, now extinct in California, or to the black bear (which is sometimes cinnamon colored). **Bear River** [Humboldt Co.] was so named because Lewis K. Wood of the Gregg party was badly mauled by a wounded grizzly here in 1850. **Bear Lake** [San Bernardino Co.] was named as early as 1845, but it is now called **Baldwin Lake;** the present **Big Bear Lake** is an artificial one created in 1884.

BEAUMONT (BOH mahnt) [Riverside Co.]. French for "beautiful mountain"; the name was given in 1887.

BECKWOURTH (BEK werth) **PASS** [Lassen, Plumas Cos.]. For James Beckwourth (also spelled Beckwith), an African American mountain man, adopted member of the Crow Indian tribe, and trailblazer of the 1840s and 1850s; he came to California in 1844.

BEEGUM PEAK [Tehama Co.]. From a southern U.S. word for "beehive"; bees actually live here, in holes in the rock.

BEL-AIR [Los Angeles Co.]. Named for its developer, Alphonso Bell, in 1923, on the model of French *bel air,* "fresh air."

BELL [Los Angeles Co.]. Named in 1898 by James George Bell and his son Alphonso, founders of the town. The place also gave its name to the nearby community of **Bell Gardens.**

BELLFLOWER [Los Angeles Co.]. Named in 1909 after an orchard of bellflower apples (from French *belle fleur,* "beautiful flower").

BELMONT [San Mateo Co.]. The name, based on Italian *bel monte* or French *beau mont,* "beautiful mountain," was applied in the 1850s.

BELVEDERE (BEL vuh deer) [Marin Co.]. Italian for "beautiful view"; applied in 1890.

BENICIA (buh NEE shuh) [Solano Co.]. This was one of the given names of the wife of General Mariano Vallejo, applied in 1847.

BEN LOMOND (ben LOH muhnd) **MOUNTAIN** [Santa Cruz Co.]. Named for the mountain that overlooks Loch Lomond in Scotland; the name is redundant, since *ben* represents the Scottish word for "mountain."

BERKELEY [Alameda Co.]. Named in 1866, by the trustees of the new university, for the Irish philosopher George Berkeley, who wrote the line "Westward the course of empire takes its way."

BERROS (BAIR ohs) [San Luis Obispo Co.]. Spanish for "watercress"; nearby **Los Berros Creek** has been so named since 1850.

BERRYESSA (bair ee YES uh) **LAKE** [Napa Co.]. For José Jesús and Sisto Berryessa, who took up land here in 1843. **Berryessa Creek** [Santa Clara Co.] is named for another family with the same surname.

BETTERAVIA (bet uh RAY vee uh) [Santa Barbara Co.]. From French *betterave,* "sugar beet," referring to the sugar-beet industry here.

BEVERLY HILLS [Los Angeles Co.]. Named in 1907 after Beverly Farms in Massachusetts, a vacation spot of then president William H. Taft.

BIDWELL STATE PARK [Butte Co.]. The park, as well as several other features in various counties, was named

for John Bidwell, who in 1841 organized the first overland party of emigrants to California; the settlers
trekked for twenty-four weeks and were forced to eat
their mules.

BIEBER (BEE ber) [Lassen Co.]. Named in 1879 for Nathan
Bieber, who ran a store here; a neighboring settlement
was later called **Nubieber.**

BIG BEAR LAKE [San Bernardino Co.]. This artificial lake,
created in 1884, borrowed the name of nearby **Bear Lake,**
now called **Baldwin Lake.** Big Bear Lake is the name not
only of the lake, but of an incorporated city; by contrast,
Big Bear City is an unincorporated community.

BIG SUR RIVER [Monterey Co.]. From Spanish Río Grande
del Sur, "big river of the south" (i.e., south of Monterey);
there is also a **Little Sur River.**

BISHOP [Inyo Co.]. Named for the cattleman Samuel A.
Bishop, who lived here in the 1860s.

BLACKHAWK [Contra Costa Co.]. Named after an American Indian chief who led native tribes of the Midwest
against the whites in the early nineteenth century.

BLACK LASSIC PEAK [Trinity Co.]. A black promontory
named after nearby **Mount Lassic,** which was named in
turn for Lassik, leader of an Athabaskan Indian tribe.

BLANCO (BLANG koh). The Spanish for "white" (fem.
blanca); it occurs in many place names, such as **Blanco
Mountain** [Mono Co.]; **Pico** (PEE koh) **Blanco** [Mon-
terey Co.], meaning "white peak"; and **Piedra** (pee AY
druh) **Blanca** [Ventura Co.], "white rock."

BLUFF. The name is used in California as a generic term
for a cliff or bank, as in **Red Bluff** [Tehama Co.]. The
stream called **Bluff Creek** [Humboldt, Del Norte Cos.]
was so named in 1851.

BLYTHE [Riverside Co.]. For Thomas H. Blythe, who in 1875 laid the plans for irrigation of the area.

BODEGA (boh DAY guh) [Sonoma Co.]. The bay was first sighted by Europeans in 1775, when the Spanish sea captain Juan Francisco de la Bodega y Quadra arrived here in his ship *Sonora;* the bay was later named for him.

BODIE (BOH dee) [Mono Co.]. The town was named for Waterman S. Body, who discovered ore deposits here in 1859; it is now a ghost town and historic landmark.

BOHEMOTASH (boh HEE muh tash) **MOUNTAIN** [Shasta Co.]. From Wintu *bohema thoos,* "big camp."

BOLINAS (boh LEE nuhs) [Marin Co.]. First recorded in 1834 as Baulenes, the name of a Coast Miwok Indian band who lived in the area. However, **Bolinas Creek** [Alameda Co.] is named for Antonio Bolena, of Portugal, who owned land here in the 1870s.

BOLLIBOKKA (bah lee BAH kuh) **MOUNTAIN** [Shasta Co.]. From Wintu *buli,* "mountain," and *phaqa,* "manzanita."

BOLLY. *See* Bally

BOLSA (BOHL suh). The Spanish word for "pocket" is used in a geographical sense—for example, for a place semienclosed by water. It occurs in many combinations, such as **Bolsa Chica** (CHEE kuh) [Orange Co.], meaning "small pocket"; and **Bolsa Knolls** [Monterey Co.].

BONITA (boh NEE tuh) [San Diego Co.]. In 1884 Henry E. Cooper named his estate Bonita Ranch, and the name was later applied to the post office. Spanish *bonita,* "pretty" (feminine), is a diminutive of *buena,* "good."

BONITA, POINT [Marin Co.]. The original Spanish was Punta Bonete, "bonnet point," because of its shape; but after 1855 this was misinterpreted as containing Spanish *bonita*, "pretty."

BONITA LAKE [Inyo Co.]. A name given by the California Department of Fish and Game, inspired by the scientific name for the golden trout, *Salmo aguabonita*, in which the species name is Spanish for "pretty water."

BONNY DOON (bah nee DOON) [Santa Cruz Co.]. The name apparently comes from a song by Robert Burns, referring to the Doon River in Scotland.

BOONVILLE [Mendocino Co.]. Named in the 1860s for the storekeeper W. W. Boone. The place has become famous for Boontling, a "secret language" invented by the inhabitants. An example of Boontling is *Kimmies japin' broadies to the airtight*, "Men are driving cows to the sawmill."

BORREGO. This Spanish word for "sheep" (fem. *borrega*) occurs in many place names; in mountain and desert areas, it may refer to the bighorn sheep. **Borrego** (buh RAY goh) **Desert** [San Diego Co.] was so named as early as 1883; the area is now part of **Anza-Borrego Desert State Park**. An alternative spelling occurs in **Borego Mountain** [San Diego Co.].

BOUQUET (boh KAY, boh KET) **CANYON** [Los Angeles Co.]. A misinterpretation of Spanish El Buque, "the ship," the nickname of a French sailor who settled there.

BRANCIFORTE (bran suh FOR tee) **CREEK** [Santa Cruz Co.]. The Pueblo de Branciforte was established in 1797, at the site of the present town of Santa Cruz, and named in honor of the viceroy of New Spain, Miguel de la Grúa Talamanco, Marquis of Branciforte. The name is now often pronounced *bran chuh FOR tee*, as if it were of Italian origin.

BRAWLEY [Imperial Co.]. Originally named Braly in 1902, for the landowner J. H. Braly. However Braly, fearing that the project would fail, asked that his name not be used; so the present spelling was substituted.

BREA (BRAY uh) [Orange Co.]. This Spanish word for "tar, asphaltum," which oozes naturally from the ground at many places in southern California, also occurs in several other place names, such as the redundantly named **La Brea Tar Pits** [Los Angeles Co.].

BRENTWOOD [Contra Costa Co.]. Named in 1878 after Brentwood in Essex, England, the ancestral home of the landowner John Marsh. The name is also applied to the **Brentwood** district in Los Angeles.

BREYFOGLE (BRAY foh guhl) **CANYON** and **BUTTES** [Death Valley N.P.]. For Charles C. Breyfogle, a famous prospector of the area. The term *breyfogling* came to be used to refer to searching for lost mines.

BRIDALVEIL FALL and **CREEK** [Yosemite N.P.]. Apparently named by a journalist in 1856.

BRIDGEPORT [Mono Co.]. Settled around 1860, and probably named for a Bridgeport in the eastern United States.

BRISBANE [San Mateo Co.]. Named in 1908 for the journalist Arthur Brisbane.

BUCHON (buh SHAHN) **POINT** [San Luis Obispo Co.]. From Spanish *buchón,* "goiter"; so named in 1769 when the Portolá expedition encountered an Indian village whose chief had a goiter.

BUELLTON [Santa Barbara Co.]. Named in 1916 for Rufus T. Buell, an early settler.

BUENA (BWAY nuh) **PARK** [Orange Co.]. Founded in 1887 and given its hybrid name (Spanish *buena,* "good").

BUENAVENTURA. Represents Spanish *buena ventura,* "good fortune"—and, as a single word, Bonaventura, the name of an Italian saint called Bonaventure in English. During the early twentieth century, many Anglo explorers applied this name to a mythical river thought to flow through central California. The saint's name in Spanish, San Buenaventura, was the original name of the city of Ventura.

BUENA VISTA [Monterey Co.]. The Spanish phrase meaning "good view" has been applied here and in many other places, such as **Buena Vista Lake** [Kern Co.].

BULLY. *See* Bally

BULLY CHOOP (bul ee CHOOP) **MOUNTAIN** [Shasta, Trinity Cos.]. Represents Wintu *buli č' uup,* "mountain peak."

BUMPASS (BUM puhs) **HELL** [Lassen N.P.]. This site of boiling mud pots and steam vents was named for Kendall V. Bumpass, a hunter, guide, and prospector of the 1860s.

BURBANK [Los Angeles Co.]. Named in 1887 for Dr. David Burbank, a Los Angeles dentist who was one of the subdividers.

BURIBURI (ber ee BER ee, byoo ree BYOO ree) **RIDGE** [San Mateo Co.]. The term is from a Costanoan Indian name, perhaps related to *purris,* "needle."

BURLINGAME [San Mateo Co.]. Named in 1868 for Anson Burlingame (1822–70), orator and diplomat.

BURNT RANCH [Trinity Co.]. So named because in 1849 Canadian miners burned down an Indian village here.

BUTANO (BYOO tuh noh, BOO tuh noh) **CREEK** [San Mateo Co.]. It is claimed that *butano* is what Spanish Californians called a drinking cup made from an animal horn.

BUTTE (BYOOT). A term borrowed from French and used in the western United States for a small isolated elevation. Butte County was named for the **Sutter Buttes** or **Marysville Buttes,** which are in what is now Sutter County.

BUTTONWILLOW [Kern Co.]. A California name for the buttonbush, which somewhat resembles a willow; a tree here was used by cowboys as a landmark.

CABAZON (KAB uh zahn) [Riverside Co.]. From Spanish *cabezón,* "big head," the name given to a local Cahuilla Indian leader.

CABRILLO (kuh BREE yoh, kuh BRIL oh) **NATIONAL MONUMENT** [San Diego Co.]. Commemorates Juan Rodriguez Cabrillo, the Portuguese navigator (in Spanish service) who in 1542 first sailed up the coast of what is now the state of California. He died and was buried in the Channel Islands.

CACHE (KASH) **CREEK** [Yolo Co.]. The name refers to a "cache" in the sense of a hiding place, from French *cacher,* "to hide." The name was given by Hudson's Bay Company trappers before 1832.

CACHUMA (kuh CHOO muh) **LAKE** [Santa Barbara Co.]. From an Indian village name that the Spanish spelled Aquitsumu, from Barbareño Chumash *aqitsuˑm,* "sign."

CAHTO (KAH toh) **CREEK** [Humboldt Co.]. Named for a tribe and language, also spelled Kato, of the Athabaskan family. The term is from Northern Pomo *khaṭo,* "lake."

CAHUENGA (kuh HUNG guh, kuh WENG guh) **PASS** [Los Angeles Co.]. From the Gabrielino village name *kawé'nga,* probably meaning "at the mountain."

CAHUILLA (kuh WEE yuh). The name of an Indian tribe living in Riverside County and of their language, which belongs to the Takic branch of the Uto-Aztecan family. The name also occurs in place names such as **Cahuilla Valley** and **Cahuilla Mountain.** *Cahuilla* is borrowed from a local Spanish term, *cahuilla,* "unbaptized Indian," used in Mission days, which is in turn apparently derived from an extinct language of Baja California. The term has sometimes been spelled Coahuilla, by confusion with the state of Coahuila in Mexico. The California place name **Coachella** [Riverside Co.] may be a variant of this same word.

CAJON (kuh HOHN) **PASS** [San Bernardino Co.]. From Spanish *cajón,* "box," used to describe a box-shaped canyon. The name of **El Cajon** [San Diego Co.] also contains this term.

CAL-. As an abbreviation of *California,* the prefix occurs in a number of names, especially near state boundaries. Thus **Calneva** (kal NEE vuh) [Lassen Co.] is close to Nevada, and **Calexico** [Imperial Co.] is on the border with Mexico.

CALABASAS (kal uh BAS uhs) [Los Angeles Co.]. From Spanish *calabazas,* "pumpkins, squashes." An alternative spelling is found in **Calabazas Creek** [Santa Clara Co.].

CALABAZAL (kal uh buh ZAHL) **CREEK** [Santa Barbara Co.]. Apparently Spanish *calabazal,* "pumpkin patch," but probably an adaptation of Ineseño Chumash *kalawashaq,* "turtle shell."

CALAVERAS (kal uh VAIR uhs) **RIVER** and **COUNTY**. From the Spanish word for "skulls," applied when a number of skeletons were found near the river around 1837. This Gold Rush area was made famous by Mark Twain's story "The Celebrated Jumping Frog of Calaveras County."

CALEXICO (kuh LEK suh koh) [Imperial Co.]. A hybrid name, coined in 1901 from *California* plus *Mexico;* its sister city across the Mexican border is called Mexicali.

CALICO HILLS [San Bernardino Co.] and CALICO PEAKS [Death Valley N.P.]. Named for desert rock formations of variegated color.

CALIENTE (kal ee EN tee, kah lee EN tee) CANYON [San Luis Obispo Co.] and RANGE [Kern Co.]. The Spanish word means "hot," and in these names is short for *agua caliente,* "hot water," or *ojo caliente,* "hot spring."

CALIFORNIA. The name was applied first to what is now called Baja California, around 1562, and later extended to Alta California, the present state of California. The term originally referred to a mythical land of Amazons, ruled by the beautiful black queen Calafia, as described in a Spanish novel, *Las sergas de Esplandián* (The exploits of Esplandian), by Garci Rodríguez de Montalvo. The term occurs in such modern names as **California City** [Kern Co.], **California Heights** [Los Angeles Co.], and **California Hot Springs** [Tulare Co.]. The Gulf of California, also known as the Sea of Cortez, is in Mexican waters, between the states of Baja California and Sonora. The term *Californio* refers to the Spanish American inhabitants of California during the Spanish and Mexican regimes.

CALIPATRIA (kal uh PAY tree uh) [Imperial Co.]. Coined in 1914 from *California* plus the Latin word *patria,* "fatherland."

CALISTOGA (kal uh STOH guh) [Napa Co.]. In 1859 Sam Brannan, the developer of the area, supposedly meant to say, "I'll make this place the Saratoga of California," referring to the resort city in New York State; but instead it came out "the Calistoga of Sarafornia."

CALLEGUAS (kah YAY guhs) **CREEK** [Ventura Co.]. From Ventureño Chumash *kayïwïsh,* "the head."

CALPELLA (kal PEL uh) [Mendocino Co.]. Named after Kalpela, chief of a Pomo Indian village. The name comes from Northern Pomo *khál phíila,* "carrying mussels down."

CALPINE [Sierra Co.]. Abbreviated from McAlpine, perhaps a family name.

CAMANCHE (kuh MAN chee) **RESERVOIR** [Calaveras Co.]. The original town site here was named in 1849 for a place in Iowa, referring to the Comanche Indian tribe of the southern Great Plains; the term is from Ute *kïmánci,* "enemy, foreigner."

CAMARILLO (kam uh RIL oh, kam uh REE yoh) [Ventura Co.]. Named for the ranch owner Juan Camarillo.

CAMBRIA (KAM bree uh, KAYM bree uh) [San Luis Obispo Co.]. Latin for "Wales"; the name was given by a Welsh carpenter in the 1860s.

CAMP. A term included in many California place names; some camps were originally military installations, while others were work sites or summer resorts. **Camp Curry** [Yosemite N.P.] was established as a resort in 1899 by David and Jennie Curry. **Camp Meeker** [Sonoma Co.] was named for Melvin C. Meeker, a lumberman.

CAMPHORA (kam FOR uh) [Monterey Co.]. Mexican railroad workers referred to Camp Four, a construction camp set up here in 1873, as Camfora.

CAMPO (KAM poh) [San Diego Co.]. The word is Spanish for "field," but in California it is often equivalent to the English word *camp.*

CAMUESA (kuh MOO suh) **PEAK** [Santa Barbara Co.]. Probably from Spanish *camuza, gamuza,* "chamois," used locally to mean "buckskin," because Indian women tanned deerskins near here.

CAMULOS (kuh MYOO luhs) [Ventura Co.]. From Ventureño Chumash *kamulus,* "the juniper."

CANDLESTICK PARK [San Francisco Co.]. Named for Candlestick Rock, an eight-foot pinnacle mapped in 1869.

CANOGA (kuh NOH guh) **PARK** [Los Angeles Co.]. Named in the 1890s after Canoga, New York, which was originally a Cayuga (Iroquoian) village.

CANYON. From Spanish *cañón,* this word forms part of many California place names, such as **Canyon** [Alameda Co.] and **Canyon Country** [Los Angeles Co.].

CAPAY (kuh PAY) [Yolo Co.]. From Hill Patwin *kapay,* "creek."

CAPITOLA (kap uh TOH luh) [Santa Cruz Co.]. The name was apparently coined from *capitol* in 1876, perhaps in the hope that the state capital would be located here.

CARDIFF-BY-THE-SEA [San Diego Co.]. Laid out in 1911 and named after the seaport in Wales.

CARLSBAD [San Diego Co.]. Named in 1886 for Karlsbad, in Bohemia (now Karlovy Vary, in the Czech Republic), because of the similarity of the mineral waters in the two places.

CARMEL (kahr MEL) **RIVER** [Monterey Co.]. The stream was discovered by Sebastián Vizcaíno in 1603 and called Río del Carmelo. Spanish *Carmelo* is the name of Mount Carmel near Jerusalem, based on Hebrew *karmel,* "vineyard, orchard." Modern applications of the name include **Carmel Valley** and the town of **Carmel-by-the-Sea**, the latter now often called simply **Carmel.**

CARPINTERIA (kahr puhn tuh REE uh) [Santa Barbara Co.]. From Spanish *carpintería,* "carpenter's shop," because the Portolá expedition found Indians building canoes here in 1769.

CARQUINEZ (kahr KEE nuhs) **STRAIT** [Solano, Contra Costa Cos.]. This is originally a Spanish plural, *Carquines,* of the Costanoan tribal name Karkin, based on a word meaning "barter."

CARRIZO (kuh REE zoh) **CREEK** [San Diego, Imperial Cos.]. Takes its name from the Spanish word for "reed grass"; California Indians used the grass to make *panoche,* similar to brown sugar. The **Carrizo Plain** [San Luis Obispo Co.] lies on the San Andreas Fault and is famous for its frequent earthquakes.

CARSON RIVER and **PASS** [Alpine Co.]. The river was named in 1848 by John C. Frémont for his guide, Christopher (Kit) Carson, a famous mountain man and Indian fighter. Carson became the hero of many dime novels and, although illiterate, dictated a best-selling autobiography. **Carson Creek** [Calaveras Co.] and the town of **Carson** [Los Angeles Co.] are named for early settlers with that surname.

CASA. The Spanish for "house" is found in some place names applied in American times, such as **Casa Blanca** (kah suh BLANG kuh) [Riverside Co.]. The site of **Casa Diablo** (dee AH bloh) [Mono Co.], for *casa del diablo,* "house of the devil," was so named because a geyser once existed there. **Casa Loma** (LOH muh) [Placer Co.] is for *casa de la loma,* "house of the hill."

CASCADE RANGE. This name applies to the range of mountains extending from Washington and Oregon south to include Lassen Peak in California; it referred earlier to the falls on the Columbia River.

CASHLAPOODA (kash luh POO duh) **CREEK** [Humboldt Co.]. Probably from the Cache la Poudre River in Colorado, French for "hide the (gun)powder"—so named by French trappers who cached their supplies there.

CASMALIA (kaz MAY lee uh) [Santa Barbara Co.]. From Purisimeño Chumash *kasma'li*, "it is the last."

CASNAU (KAZ naw) **CREEK** [Tuolumne Co.]. Sometimes thought to be named for General Thomas N. Casneau or Casnau, but in fact named for Thomas Casenave, a French rancher who received a patent here in 1875.

CASTAIC (kas TAYK) [Los Angeles Co.]. From Ventureño Chumash *kashtiq*, "the eye, the face." An alternative spelling is used for **Castac Lake** and **Valley** [Kern Co.].

CASTRO. A common Spanish surname, used to name several places in California. **Castro Valley** [Alameda Co.] was named for the early landowner Guillermo Castro. **Castroville** [Monterey Co.] was laid out and named in 1864 by Juan Bautista Castro.

CAYUCOS (kah YOO kuhs) [San Luis Obispo Co.]. The plural of Spanish *cayuco*, "fishing canoe," borrowed from Eskimo *kayak*.

CAZADERO (kaz uh DAIR oh) [Sonoma Co.]. Spanish for "hunting place," named in the late 1880s.

CECILVILLE [Siskiyou Co.]. Contains a misspelling of the name of the pioneer John Baker Sissel.

CENTINELA (sen tuh NEL uh) **CREEK** [Los Angeles Co.]. From the Spanish word for "sentry, sentinel." The name **Santa Nella** [Merced Co.] is from the same origin.

CENTRAL VALLEY. The area encompassed by the Sacramento and San Joaquin Valleys in central California. The town of **Central Valley** [Shasta Co.] was named in 1938 for the Central Valley Project, which built Shasta Dam.

CENTURY CITY [Los Angeles Co.]. Named for 20th Century-Fox film studios, on the site of which it was built, starting in 1961.

CERES (SEER eez) [Stanislaus Co.]. Named for the Roman goddess of agriculture.

CERRITO. Spanish for "little hill" (diminutive of *cerro*, "hill"), it is the basis for several place names, such as **Cerritos** (suh REE tohs) [Los Angeles Co.] and **El Cerrito** [Contra Costa Co.]. The "little hill" of the latter is actually in the neighboring town of Albany and is known as Albany Hill.

CHAGOOPA (chuh GOO puh) FALLS [Sequoia N.P.]. Supposedly named for an old Paiute chief.

CHALANEY (chuh LAY nee) CREEK [Tulare Co.]. Previously known as Chilean Creek and Chanley Creek; it is possibly from Spanish *chileno*, "Chilean," because of Chilean miners who participated in the Gold Rush.

CHALONE (shuh LOHN, chuh LOHN) [San Benito, Monterey Cos.]. Represents a Costanoan place name, *čalon*, of unknown meaning.

CHAMISE (shuh MEES, chuh MEES). With the variant spelling Chemise, refers to various kinds of brushwood, including the greasewood bush; it is from Spanish *chamiso. Chamisal* is Spanish for a place where chamise grows; in English it is also spelled Chemisal. These two terms occur in place names such as **Chemise Creek** [Mendocino Co.] and **Chemisal Ridge** [Monterey Co.].

CHANCHELULLA (chan chuh LOO luh) MOUNTAIN [Trinity Co.]. From Wintu *son čuluula*, literally, "rock black."

CHANNEL ISLANDS. The collective name for the islands that are separated from the mainland by the Santa Barbara Channel, including Santa Catalina, San Miguel, Santa Rosa, and Santa Cruz.

CHATSWORTH [Los Angeles Co.]. Named in 1887 after the estate of the Duke of Devonshire in England.

CHATTERDOWEN (CHAT er dow uhn) **CREEK** [Shasta Co.]. From Wintu *čati tawin*, literally, "digger pine-nut flat."

CHEMEHUEVI (CHEM uh way vee). The name of an Indian tribe of San Bernardino County and their language, which belongs to the Numic branch of the Uto-Aztecan family; the term also occurs in place names such as **Chemehuevi Valley**. The name of the tribe is apparently derived from their name in the neighboring Mojave language: *'achiimuuév*, "those who work with fish."

CHEROKEE (CHAIR uh kee). During the Gold Rush, several mining camps were named for members of this Indian tribe from the southeastern United States who came to try their luck in California. The tribe's name for themselves is *tsalagi*, of unknown origin.

CHICKABALLY (CHIK uh bah lee) **MOUNTAIN** [Shasta Co.]. Probably from Wintu *likup'uri*, "a fight," merged with *buli*, "mountain."

CHICO (CHEE koh) [Butte Co.]. Spanish for "small," abbreviated from the name of the land grant Arroyo Chico, "small stream." **Chico Creek** has two tributaries, called **Big Chico Creek** (literally, "big small creek") and **Little Chico Creek** ("small small creek").

CHILAO (chuh LAY oh) [Los Angeles Co.]. Formerly Chileo or Chilleo, a nickname of the herder José Gonzales, famous for killing a grizzly bear near here with only a hunting knife. The nickname may be from Spanish *chileno,* "Chilean."

CHILENO (chuh LAY noh) VALLEY [Marin Co.]. From the Spanish word for a native of Chile. The presence of Chilean miners during the Gold Rush gave rise to several California place names.

CHINA. As a part of California place names, this word reflects the role of Chinese workers in the Gold Rush and in the later history of the state. **China Basin** [San Francisco Co.] was named for the "China clippers," ships that docked here in the 1860s.

CHINO (CHEE noh) [San Bernardino Co.]. The name given by the Spanish to a local Indian leader. The Spanish word *chino* means "Chinese," but it is also used in Mexico for a person of mixed race.

CHINQUAPIN (CHING kuh pin) [Yosemite N.P.]. Named for a nut-bearing bush. The word is originally from a Virginia Algonquian language and was introduced into English by Captain John Smith in 1612.

CHIQUITO (chuh KEE toh) CREEK [Madera Co.]. Spanish for "little" (diminutive of *chico*), an abbreviation of Chiquito Joaquín, "little [San] Joaquin [River]."

CHIRPCHATTER MOUNTAIN [Shasta Co.]. From Wintu *t'arap č'araw,* literally, "cottonwood field," from *t'arap,* "cottonwood tree," plus *č'araw,* "green place."

CHISMAHOO (CHIS muh hoo) CREEK [Ventura Co.]. Probably from Ventureño Chumash *ts'ismuhu,* "it streams out."

CHOLAME (shoh LAM, choh LAM) [San Luis Obispo Co.]. The name of a Salinan Indian village; it is from Migueleño Salinan *č'olám,* said to refer to evil people.

CHOWCHILLA (chow CHIL uh) **RIVER** [Madera, Mariposa Cos.]. From the name of a Yokuts Indian tribe whom the Spanish called Chauciles. The name was also applied to a neighboring Miwok group.

CHUAL (CHOO uhl), **MOUNT** [Santa Clara Co.]. The term is Mexican Spanish for "pigweed," from Aztec *tzoalli*. **Chualar** (choo uh LAHR) [Monterey Co.] is Mexican Spanish for "place where *chual* grows."

CHUCHUPATE (choo choo PAT ee) [Kern Co.]. The Mexican Spanish name for a wild herb, derived from Aztec *xoxouhca-pahtli* (literally, "blue medicine").

CHUCKAWALLA (CHUK wah luh) **MOUNTAIN** [Riverside Co.]. The name of a desert lizard, also spelled chuckwalla; the word comes from Cahuilla *cháxwal*.

CHUCKCHANSI (chuk CHAN see). Refers to a tribe and language of the Yokuts family, and to the Indian reservation now occupied by the group [Fresno Co.]. The original Yokuts name is *čhukčhansi,* of uncertain meaning.

CHULA VISTA (choo luh VIS tuh) [San Diego Co.]. The name, applied in 1888, is intended to be Spanish for "pretty view."

CHUMASH (CHOO mash). A cover term for several related tribes and languages of San Luis Obispo, Santa Barbara, and Ventura Counties—famous for their seagoing canoes, made of rough-hewn planks, drilled and sewn together with vines, then caulked with asphalt. Different groups are distinguished by their mission associations, such as Obispeño, Purisimeño, Ineseño, and Barbareño. *Chumash* originally referred to the group living on the Channel Islands. All the Chumashan languages are now extinct. There is a **Chumash Peak** in San Luis Obispo County.

CIENEGA (see EN uh guh) CREEK [San Benito Co.]. The Spanish term *ciénega* (with the alternative form *ciénaga*) refers to a marsh or a marshy meadow. It occurs in a variety of place names, including **Cienaga Seca** (SAY kuh) [San Bernardino Co.], meaning "dry meadow," and **La Cienega Boulevard** in Los Angeles.

CISCO [Placer Co.]. Named by the Central Pacific Railroad in honor of John J. Cisco, treasurer of the company.

CLEAR LAKE [Lake Co.]. Called Laguna Grande, "big lake," in Spanish times; the present name first appeared in 1851.

CLEVELAND NATIONAL FOREST [Orange, Riverside, San Diego Cos.]. Named in 1908 in memory of President Grover Cleveland, a week after his death.

CLIKAPUDI (KLIK uh poo dee) CREEK [Shasta Co.]. From Wintu *likup'uri,* "a fight."

CLOVIS (KLOH vuhs) [Fresno Co.]. Named in 1889 for the ranch owner Clovis Cole.

COACHELLA (koh CHEL uh, koh uh CHEL uh) VALLEY [Riverside Co.]. Earlier called the Cahuilla Valley, after the Indian tribe. The change to Coachella around 1900 may have been influenced by confusion with Spanish *conchilla,* "little shell."

COALINGA (koh uh LING guh) [Fresno Co.]. Originally called Coaling Station by the Southern Pacific Railway; the name was then Hispanicized by combining *coaling* with -*a*.

COCHES (KOH chuhs) CANYON [San Diego Co.]. From a Mexican Spanish word for "pigs."

COCOPA (KOH koh pah). The name of an Indian tribe living in Imperial County and in adjacent areas of Arizona and Mexico, and their language, which belongs to

the Yuman family; their name for themselves is *kokwapá*.
The **Cocopah Mountains** are named for this tribe.

COLFAX [Placer Co.]. Named in 1865 in honor of the visit
of Schuyler Colfax, then Speaker of the U.S. House of
Representatives.

COLLAYOMI (kah lee YOH mee) VALLEY [Lake Co.].
Probably reflects a Spanish spelling of Lake Miwok
koyáa-yomi, "song place."

COLMA (KOHL muh) [San Mateo Co.]. The name dates
from 1872 and may be from the town of Colma in
Switzerland. However, in the San Francisco dialect of the
Costanoan Indians, *kolma* means "moon."

COLOMA (kuh LOH muh) [El Dorado Co.]. From the
name of a Nisenan (Southern Maidu) village, given in
1848 as Culloma. The town grew up around Sutter's mill
after the discovery of gold in 1848.

COLORADO (kah luh RAD oh) RIVER. The Spanish term
meaning "red" was applied to the river in 1604, during
the exploration of Arizona, referring to the reddish-
brown color of the water. The river forms the boundary
between California and Arizona; the state of Colorado is
so named because the headwaters of the river are there.

COLTON [San Bernardino Co.]. Named in 1875 for David
D. Colton, an official of the Central Pacific Railroad.

COLUMBIA [Tuolumne Co.]. The name of this historic
Gold Rush town, now reconstructed and restored as a
state park, reflects the poetic term for America, derived
from the name of Columbus.

COLUSA (kuh LOO suh). The name of a Patwin Indian
village, recorded in 1821 as Coru. The town and county
were founded in 1850 with the name Colusi, which was
changed to its present form in 1854.

COMPTCHE (KAHMP chee) [Mendocino Co.]. Probably an Indian name, possibly from the Pomo village *koma-cho*.

COMPTON [Los Angeles Co.]. Laid out in 1869, as a Methodist temperance colony, by Griffith D. Compton.

CONCEPTION (kuhn SEP shun), **POINT** [Santa Barbara Co.]. From Spanish *concepción;* named by Vizcaíno in 1602 in honor of the Immaculate Conception of the Virgin Mary (i.e., the conception of Mary, not of Jesus).

CONCORD [Contra Costa Co.]. Although founded in 1862 as Todos Santos (all saints), by 1869 it had been renamed after Concord, Massachusetts.

CONCOW (KON kow, KONG kow) **CREEK** [Butte Co.]. Named for the Concow Indians, a branch of the Maidu; their name in their language is *koyoom k'awi,* "valley earth."

CONEJO (kuh NAY hoh, kuh NAY oh) **VALLEY** [Ventura Co.]. From the Spanish word for "rabbit"; it was mentioned as a place name in 1776.

CONTRA COSTA (kahn truh KOH stuh, . . . KAW stuh) **COUNTY.** From a term used by the Spanish, from 1797 onward, to designate the "opposite coast" from San Francisco.

CONVICT CREEK and **LAKE** [Mono Co.]. In 1871 a posse fought here with convicts who had escaped from Carson City, Nevada.

COPCO [Siskiyou Co.]. Coined in 1915 from *C*alifornia *O*regon *P*ower *Co*mpany, which built a hydroelectric project here.

CORNING [Tehama Co.]. Named in 1882 in memory of John Corning, an official of the Central Pacific Railroad, who had died in 1878.

CORONA (kuh ROH nuh) [Riverside Co.]. Latin or Spanish for "crown"; it was applied to the town in 1896. **Corona del Mar** [Orange Co.], "crown of the sea," was named in 1904.

CORONADO (kor uh NAH doh) [San Diego Co.]. Named in 1887 after the Coronado Islands, off the coast of Baja California. These had been named by the Spanish in 1602 after Los Cuatro Coronados, "the four crowned ones," Roman martyrs of early Christianity.

CORRAL (kuh RAL). The Spanish word for "enclosure" is used in the western United States to designate a pen for livestock and appears in many place names. **Corral Canyon** [Los Angeles Co.] has given its name to the adjoining beach—which is, however, often reinterpreted as "Coral Beach." **Corralitos** (kor uh LEE tuhs) [Santa Cruz Co.] is the diminutive form, "little corrals."

CORTE MADERA (kor tee muh DAIR uh, kor tuh . . .) [Marin Co.]. From Spanish *corte de madera,* "a place where wood is cut," referring to John Reed's sawmill.

COSO (KOH soh) [Inyo Co.]. Probably from the local Panamint Indian language, in which *kosoowa* means "be steamy," referring to hot springs in the area. In the 1860s a Coso County was proposed, but it was superseded by Inyo County.

COSTA MESA (koh stuh MAY suh) [Orange Co.]. An Americanized combination of Spanish *costa,* "coast," plus *mesa,* "table, tableland."

COSTANOAN (kah stuh NOH uhn). A cover term referring to a group of related Indian tribes and their languages, which were once spoken in Contra Costa, Alameda, San Francisco, San Mateo, Santa Clara, San Benito, Santa Cruz, and Monterey Counties; all these languages are now extinct. The term is from Spanish *costano,* "belonging to the coast." Various Costanoan groups go by the names of Ohlone, Mutsun, and Rumsen.

COSUMNES (kuh SUM nuhs) RIVER [El Dorado, Sacramento Cos.]. From the name of an Indian group, probably from Plains Miwok *kooso,* "toyon berries" (sometimes called California holly).

COTATI (koh TAH tee) [Sonoma Co.]. From *kotati,* the name of a Coast Miwok Indian village.

COTTANEVA (kah tuh NEE vuh) CREEK [Mendocino Co.]. Probably named from Kato (Athabaskan) *kaatəneebi,* "place where the trail goes over the hill."

COUTOLENC (KOH tuh links) [Butte Co.]. Originally Coutolanezes, for a settler named Eugene Coutolanezes. Abbreviated to the present form when a post office was established here in the 1880s.

COVELO (KOH vuh loh) [Mendocino Co.]. Named around 1870, probably for Covolo in Italy or Covelo in Spain.

COVINA (koh VEE nuh) [Los Angeles Co.]. Dates from the late 1880s; the name was apparently adopted simply because of its pleasant sound, with an echo of Spanish *viña,* "vineyard."

COW HOLLOW [San Francisco Co.]. So named for its dairies (ca. 1860–80), it is now a fashionable residential and shopping area.

COYOTE (kah YOH tee) RIVER [Santa Clara Co.]. The stream was named in 1776. The animal figures as a world maker and trickster in the myths of many western Indian tribes. The Spanish word is borrowed from Aztec *coyotl;* it occurs in many other place names, such as **Los Coyotes**

[San Diego Co.] and **Coyote Wells** [Imperial Co.]. The pronunciation *KAH yoht* is used in some areas outside California.

CRESCENT CITY [Del Norte Co.]. Named in 1853 because of its crescent-shaped bay. The central part of town was reconstructed after its destruction in a 1964 tidal wave that originated in Alaska. In Los Angeles County there are two fanciful place names apparently based on *crescent:* **La Crescenta,** which is faux Spanish (real Spanish would be *la creciente*), and **Crescentia,** perhaps suggested by the botanical name of the tropical calabash tree, *Crescentia cujete,* now grown in southern California.

CROCKETT [Contra Costa Co.]. Named in 1881 for Judge J. B. Crockett, who became owner of the land when he was given eighteen hundred acres in payment for settling a lawsuit.

CUASLUI (kwahs LIE) CREEK [Santa Barbara Co.]. From Spanish *guaslay,* taken from Purisimeño Chumash *awashla'y,* "net sack."

CUCAMONGA (koo kuh MUNG guh) [San Bernardino Co.]. From the Gabrielino Indian place name *kúka-monga,* of unknown meaning.

CUESTA (KWES tuh) PASS [San Luis Obispo Co.]. From the Spanish word for "slope, grade," referring to the route across the Santa Lucia Mountains.

CULVER CITY [Los Angeles Co.]. Named for Harry H. Culver, who subdivided the area in 1914.

CUPEÑO (koo PAYN yoh). A tribe living in San Diego County, and their language, which belongs to the Takic branch of the Uto-Aztecan family. The name is Spanish, derived from *kúpa,* the name of the Cupeño home village at Warner Springs.

CUPERTINO (koo per TEE noh) [Santa Clara Co.]. Named for Saint Joseph of Cupertino, an Italian saint of the seventeenth century.

CUYAMA (kwee YAH muh) **RIVER** [Santa Barbara, San Luis Obispo Cos.]. From the name of an Indian village, from Chumash *kuyam,* "clam," referring to a freshwater mollusk. Alternative pronunciations are *koo YAH muh* and *kwee YAM uh.*

CUYAMACA (kwee yuh MAK uh, koo yuh MAK uh, koo yuh MAH kuh) [San Diego Co.]. From Diegueño *'ekwiiyemak,* "behind the clouds."

CUYAPIPE or **CUYAPAIPA** (koo yuh PIPE, kwee ya PIE puh) **INDIAN RESERVATION** [San Diego Co.]. From Diegueño *'ewiiyaapaayp,* "leaning rock"; also spelled Guyapipe.

DALY CITY [San Mateo Co.]. The settlement came into existence when many people found a refuge there after the San Francisco earthquake and fire of 1906. It was incorporated in 1911 and named for John Daly, a local dairyman.

DANA (DAY nuh) **POINT** [Orange Co.]. Named in 1884 for Richard Henry Dana, the author of *Two Years before the Mast,* who as a sailor visited California in 1835–36. Near here Dana swung over a cliff on halyards to dislodge some cowhides that fellow sailors were trying to throw onto the beach below.

DANTES VIEW [Death Valley N.P.]. So named after Dante's description of Hell in the *Divine Comedy.*

DANVILLE [Contra Costa Co.]. Named in the 1860s, possibly after Danville, Kentucky.

DARDANELLES (dahr duh NELZ), **THE** [Alpine, Tuolumne Cos.]. Apparently named because the peaks were reminiscent of mountain castles that guard the entrance to the Dardanelles strait in Turkey, connecting the Aegean Sea with the Sea of Marmara.

DARWIN, MOUNT [Kings Canyon N.P.]. Named in 1895 for Charles Darwin, famous for the theory of evolution. But **Darwin Canyon** [Inyo Co.] was named in 1860 for Dr. Darwin French, who searched for gold in the area.

DAVIDSON, MOUNT [San Francisco Co.]. Named in 1912 for the astronomer George Davidson.

DAVIS [Yolo Co.]. Named for Jerome C. Davis, a rancher of the 1850s.

DEATH VALLEY [Inyo, San Bernardino Cos.]. So named by gold seekers in the 1850s, from its forbidding appearance and because of the skeletal remains of unfortunate travelers who died there of heat and thirst.

DELANO (duh LAY noh) [Kern Co.]. Named in 1873 for Columbus Delano, at that time U.S. Secretary of the Interior; in recent times it became well known as the center of the United Farm Workers union under Cesar Chavez.

DELGADA (del GAY duh), **POINT** [Humboldt Co.]. The Spanish name Punta Delgada, "narrow point," was applied by Bodega in 1775.

DEL MAR [San Diego Co.]. The Spanish name, meaning "of the sea," was given in 1884, inspired by Bayard Taylor's poem "The Fight of Paso del Mar."

DEL MONTE (del MAHN tee) [Monterey Co.]. The name, meaning "of the forest," was first applied to the hotel in 1886, echoing the name Monterey. Spanish *monte* originally meant "mountain" but in modern usage generally means "forest, brush." Anglo inventors of place names in California have often taken it to mean "mountain."

DEL NORTE (del NORT) **COUNTY**. Named by the state legislature in 1857, from the Spanish phrase meaning "of the north."

DELONEGHA (duh LAH nuh guh) **HOT SPRINGS** [Kern Co.]. Takes its name from Dahlonega, Georgia, once a gold-mining center; it is derived in turn from Cherokee *adel dalonige,* "money yellow"—that is, gold.

DELTA. The name is applied loosely to the wetlands area in the Central Valley where the San Joaquin and Sacramento Rivers join and flow into San Pablo Bay.

DE LUZ (duh LOOZ) [San Diego Co.]. Spanish for "of light"; but the town was actually named for a pioneer farmer surnamed Luce.

DESCANSO (duhs KAN soh) [San Diego Co.]. Named in 1877 from the Spanish word for "rest, repose."

DEVIL. A term appearing in many place names, generally referring to places of dangerous or infernal aspect. **Devils Postpile** [Madera Co.] is a strange pile of basalt columns, set aside as a national monument in 1911. **Devils Golf Course** [Death Valley N.P.] is an expanse of jagged salt hummocks on which only the devil could play golf.

DIABLO (die AB loh, dee AB loh, dee AHB loh), **MOUNT** [Contra Costa Co.]. The name Monte del Diablo, "devil's woods," was applied to an area near Concord around 1824. At a later date, Anglo explorers interpreted the name as "devil's mountain" and applied it to the nearby peak. The bizarre combination San Diablo, "saint devil," is now occasionally heard, whether in joke or in error.

DIDALLAS (die DAL uhs) **CREEK** [Shasta Co.]. From Wintu *didalas,* "daybreak."

DIEGUEÑO (dee uh GAYN yoh). Refers to an Indian tribe living in San Diego County and the adjacent area of Mexico, and their language, which belongs to the Yuman family; portions of the tribe are also called Ipai, Tipai, and Kumeyaay. The term *Diegueño* is Spanish, derived from the name of San Diego Mission.

DINKEY CREEK [Fresno Co.]. Named in 1863 by hunters whose dog Dinkey was injured there in a fight with a grizzly bear.

DINUBA (duh NOO buh) [Tulare Co.]. May be a fanciful name invented by a construction engineer of the Southern Pacific Railway.

DIXON [Solano Co.]. Named in 1870 for Thomas Dickson, with a misspelling introduced by the Post Office Department.

DOLORES, MISSION [San Francisco Co.]. This common designation of the San Francisco mission is from the name Nuestra Señora de los Dolores, "Our Lady of Sorrows," given by Anza in 1776 to a nearby stream.

DOMINGUEZ (duh MING guhz) **HILLS** [Los Angeles Co.]. Named for the rancho granted to Juan José Domínguez around 1784. The name **Laguna Dominguez** was given in 1938 to a nearby swamp previously known as Nigger Slough.

DONNER LAKE and **PASS** [Nevada, Placer Cos.]. These names commemorate the party of pioneers, led by George and Jacob Donner, who were forced to winter here in 1846–47; thirty-six people died of cold and starvation, and some resorted to cannibalism.

DOS PALOS (daws PAL ohs) [Merced Co.]. Spanish for "two trees." The word *palo,* meaning "stick, wood," has often been used in California to mean "tree," as in **Palo Alto**, "tall tree."

DOS RIOS (daws REE ohs) [Mendocino Co.]. Spanish for "two rivers"; so named because the town is located where two branches of the Eel River meet.

DOWNEY [Los Angeles Co.]. Named in 1865 for John G. Downey, who had earlier been governor of California.

DOWNIEVILLE [Sierra Co.]. Named for William Downie, a Scottish miner during the Gold Rush.

DRAKES BAY [Marin Co.]. Named for the English explorer Sir Francis Drake, who visited the coast of northern California in 1579. However, there is no evidence that Drake actually anchored in this bay.

DUARTE (doo AHR tee, DWAHR tee) [Los Angeles Co.]. Named for Andrés Duarte, whose ranch here was subdivided in 1864–65.

DUBAKELLA (DOO buh kel uh) **MOUNTAIN** [Trinity Co.]. From Wintu *duubit kiili,* the name of a type of edible root locally called a wild potato.

DUBLIN [Alameda Co.]. Named in the 1860s, probably because many Irish lived in the area.

DUCOR (DOO kor) [Tulare Co.]. An abbreviation of Dutch Corners, so called in 1899 because four German families had adjoining homesteads here. Germans were formerly often called "Dutch" in the United States, reflecting the German adjective *deutsch,* "German."

DULZURA (duhl ZOOR uh) [San Diego Co.]. Spanish for "sweetness," from *dulce,* "sweet."

DUMBARTON BRIDGE [Alameda, San Mateo Cos.]. Named in 1876 for what was then a county in Scotland.

DUME (DOOM, doo MAY), **POINT** [Los Angeles Co.].
The name was given to the cape by George Vancouver in
1793, in honor of Padre Francisco Dumetz of Mission San
Buenaventura; but it was misspelled as Dume on Vancouver's map and has never been corrected.

DUNSMUIR [Siskiyou Co.]. Named in 1886 for Alexander Dunsmuir, a coal magnate of San Francisco who
promised the townspeople a fountain if they would name
the town after him.

EAGLE ROCK [Los Angeles Co.]. So named because the
shadow of the rock resembles the outline of an eagle.

EARL, LAKE [Del Norte Co.]. From a Yurok place name,
rrł. There was no Mr. Earl.

EARLIMART [Tulare Co.]. So named in 1909 to indicate
that crops mature early there.

EDWARDS AIR FORCE BASE [Kern Co.]. Formerly Muroc
Air Field, it received its present name in 1950 in memory
of Captain Glenn W. Edwards, who was fatally injured in
a crash here.

EEL RIVER [Mendocino, Humboldt Cos.]. Named in 1850
by Josiah Gregg's exploring party, after they obtained a
large number of eels from Indians in trade for a broken
frying pan.

EL CAJON (kuh HOHN) [San Diego Co.]. Spanish *el cajón* means "the box"; the area was so called because the
site is enclosed by hills.

EL CAPITAN (KAP uh tan, kap uh TAN, kah puh TAHN)
[Yosemite N.P.]. Spanish *el capitán* means "the captain,
the chief"; the name was intended as a translation for the
Indian name of this towering cliff.

EL CENTRO [Imperial Co.]. Spanish for "the center"; the town was so called in 1905 because of its location in the Imperial Valley.

EL CERRITO (suh REE toh) [Contra Costa Co.]. Spanish for "the little hill," diminutive of *cerro;* the name was applied to the isolated knoll at the bay shore now called Albany Hill, which is part of the city of Albany.

EL DORADO. The Spanish term, meaning "the gilded one," first appears in Colombia in the sixteenth century, referring to a mythical Indian chief who was supposedly covered with gold during religious rites. Subsequently the name designated one of the golden utopias sought by the Spanish conquistadors in Latin America. With the beginning of the Gold Rush in California, the term had a new context, and it was applied to **El Dorado County** in 1850.

EL GRANADA (gruh NAH duh) [San Mateo Co.]. So named in 1910, perhaps for the city in Spain; however, the masculine article *el* is ungrammatical here.

ELK. This animal, once common in California, is mentioned in many place names. **Elk Grove** [Sacramento Co.] takes its name from the Elk Grove House, a hotel of 1850 with an elk's head painted over the door.

EL MODENA (muh DEE nuh) [Orange Co.]. The settlement was named after the Italian city Modena (which has the accent on the first syllable). However, the Spanish masculine article *el* is ungrammatical here.

EL MONTE (MAHN tee) [Los Angeles Co.]. Spanish not for "the mountain" (the city is on a plain), but rather for "the woods, the brush"; so called in 1852 because of a dense stand of willows.

ELMS CANYON [Los Angeles Co.]. Named in 1882 or 1883 for Dr. Henry Elms, owner of the land at the mouth of the canyon.

EL SEGUNDO (suh GUN doh, suh GUHN doh) [Los Angeles Co.]. Spanish for "the second," applied in 1911 because it was the second refinery of the Standard Oil Company in California.

ELSINORE, LAKE [Riverside Co.]. The name was given in 1884, after the Danish city that provides the setting for Shakespeare's *Hamlet.*

EL SOBRANTE (suh BRAHN tee) [Contra Costa Co.]. The Spanish word *sobrante* refers to an area left over after a land grant has been surveyed. A local joke is that the name means "the leftovers."

ELTERPOM (EL tuh pahm) **CREEK** [Trinity Co.]. From Wintu *eltipom,* "place on the other side."

EL TORO (TOR oh) [Orange Co.]. Spanish for "the bull"; the name was applied around 1838.

EMBARCADERO (em bahr kuh DAIR oh) [San Francisco Co.]. Spanish for "embarking place, wharf, dock."

EMERYVILLE [Alameda Co.]. Named in 1897 for the landowner Joseph S. Emery.

EMIGRANT GAP [Placer Co.]. Refers to a route taken by the wagon trains of settlers who traveled overland to California in the years after the Gold Rush.

ENCANTO (en KAN toh) [San Diego Co.]. The Spanish word for "enchantment" was applied around 1910.

ENCINITAS (en suh NEE tuhs) [San Diego Co.]. Spanish for "little live oaks," plural diminutive of *encina.*

ENCINO (en SEE noh) [Los Angeles Co.]. Also a variant of *encina,* "live oak"; the name was applied here around

1840. Spanish distinguishes *encina,* the live oak, from *roble,* the deciduous oak.

ESCONDIDO (es kuhn DEE doh) [San Diego Co.]. Spanish for "hidden"; the name was given to the town in 1885.

ESPERANZA (es puh RAHN zuh) **CREEK** [Calaveras Co.]. From the Spanish word for "hope," which is also used as a woman's name.

ESQUON (ES kwahn) [Butte Co.]. From the name of a Konkow (Northwestern Maidu) village, *eskeni.*

ESSELEN (ES uh luhn). The name of an Indian tribe and their language, once spoken on the coast of Monterey County. The term was used in recent years to name the **Esalen Institute,** an educational foundation at Big Sur, considered the birthplace of the human-potential movement.

ESTERO (es TAIR oh) **BAY** and **POINT** [San Luis Obispo Co.]. From the Spanish word for the estuary of a river. **Estero de Limantour** [Marin Co.] is named for José Yves Limantour, a Frenchman resident in Mexico who in the 1850s used forged documents to claim ownership of much valuable property in the San Francisco area. By the time the fraud was discovered, Limantour had cashed in his holdings and fled to Mexico.

ESTRELLA (es TRAY yuh) **CREEK** [San Luis Obispo Co.]. From the Spanish word for "star," also used as a woman's name.

ETIWANDA (et uh WAHN duh) [San Bernardino Co.]. Named in 1882 for the chief of an unidentified Indian tribe near Lake Michigan.

ETNA [Siskiyou Co.]. Also spelled Aetna, it takes its name from the volcanic mountain in Sicily.

ETTAWA (ET uh wuh) [Lake Co.]. Perhaps from Lake Miwok *éetaw*, "hot"; or it may have been coined by a local landowner from the name of his mother, Etta Waughtel.

ETTERSBURG [Humboldt Co.]. Named in 1894 for the horticulturist Albert F. Etter.

EUREKA (yoo REE kuh) [Humboldt Co.]. Ancient Greek for "I have found it." According to legend, the mathematician Archimedes once solved a problem while in his bath, and leaped out crying "Eureka!" It became the motto of the state of California in 1849 and was applied to the city in 1850.

EXETER [Tulare Co.]. Named in 1880 for the founder's home city in England.

FAIRFAX [Marin Co.]. Named for Charles Snowden Fairfax, popularly styled Lord Fairfax, of Fairfax County, Virginia, who settled here in 1856.

FAIRFIELD [Solano Co.]. Named in 1859 by the clippership captain Robert Waterman after his former home in Connecticut.

FALLBROOK [San Diego Co.]. Named in 1859 for Fallbrook, Pennsylvania.

FALL RIVER [Shasta Co.]. So named by John C. Frémont in 1846 because of its cascades.

FANDANGO VALLEY [Modoc Co.]. The name of a Spanish dance was supposedly given in the winter of 1849, when a party of travelers had to dance all night to keep warm.

FARALLON (FAIR uh lahn, FAIR uh lohn) **ISLANDS** [San Francisco Co.]. From Spanish *farallón*, "small rocky island"; the term was applied here in 1603.

FEATHER RIVER [Butte, Plumas Cos.]. The name was given by Hudson's Bay Company trappers in the 1830s. In later years Sutter claimed that he had given the name in the 1840s—along with its Spanish equivalent, Río de las Plumas, from which the name of Plumas County is derived.

FELTON [Santa Cruz Co.]. Named in 1878 for John Brooks Felton, who had represented California in Congress.

FERMIN (FER muhn), **POINT** [Los Angeles Co.]. Named by George Vancouver in 1793, in honor of Padre Fermín Francisco de Lasuén.

FERNANDEZ PASS [Yosemite N.P.]. Named for Joseph Fernandez, a soldier in the Fourth Cavalry, who explored the area in 1895–97.

FERNDALE [Humboldt Co.]. Named about 1870 for the luxuriant growth of ferns in the redwood belt.

FIDDLETOWN [Amador Co.]. Settled in 1849 by miners from Missouri; supposedly many of them played fiddles for entertainment.

FILLMORE [Ventura Co.]. Named in 1887 for J. A. Fillmore, a Southern Pacific railway executive.

FIREBAUGH (FIRE baw) [Fresno Co.]. A misspelling of the name of A. D. Fierbaugh, who established a trading post here in 1854.

FLINTRIDGE [Los Angeles Co.]. Named in 1920 for U.S. senator Frank P. Flint. In 1979 a merger of the town with La Cañada produced the combined name **La Cañada Flintridge.**

FLORES (FLOR uhs) **PEAK** [Orange Co.]. Named for the bandit Juan Flores, who was captured here in 1857 by a band of vigilantes, taken to Los Angeles, and hanged.

FOLSOM (FOHL suhm) [Sacramento Co.]. Named in 1855 for Joseph L. Folsom, owner of the rancho where the settlement was established.

FONTANA (fahn TAN uh) [San Bernardino Co.]. May be a family name, or a Spanish poetic word for "fountain."

FORK. As a geographical term, this refers to a branch of a river, such as the North and South Forks of the Salmon River [Siskiyou Co.] or the Fish Fork of the San Gabriel River [Los Angeles Co.]. The terminology has sometimes been overused, producing monstrosities such as "the West Fork of the South Fork of the North Fork of the San Joaquin River."

FORT BRAGG [Mendocino Co.]. Established as a military post in 1857 and named after Braxton Bragg, an officer in the Mexican War and in the Confederate Army during the Civil War.

FORT JONES [Siskiyou Co.]. The fort was named in 1852 for Colonel Roger Jones, then adjutant general of the U.S. Army.

FORT ROSS [Sonoma Co.]. Founded by Russians in 1812; the old Russian fort and church have been reconstructed in the present state park. *Ross* is a poetic name for "Russian" in the Russian language.

FORTUNA (for TOO nuh) [Humboldt Co.]. The town was founded in the 1870s and given the name Fortune, which was later changed to the present Latin form.

FRAZIER MOUNTAIN [Ventura Co.]. Named for William T. Frazer, who mined in this area from 1852. This surname, from French *fraisier,* "strawberry merchant," fluctuates in English between the spellings Fraser, Frazer, Frasier, and Frazier, pronounced with both *z* and *zh*.

FREMONT (FREE mahnt) [Alameda Co.]. Named for the explorer John C. Frémont, adored by the public for his romantic spirit of derring-do, who raised the Stars and Stripes over California in 1846. While he was in the U.S. Army, his defiant style led him to be court-martialed and convicted of mutiny, but after receiving a presidential pardon, he served as a U.S. senator from California, and in 1856 he became the first Republican candidate for president. In 1956 the towns of Centerville, Niles, Irvington, Mission San Jose, and Warm Springs united to form the city with this name.

FRESNO (FREZ noh). Spanish for "ash tree." The **Fresno River** [Madera Co.] was so called in 1851. **Fresno County** was created in 1856, and the city of **Fresno** soon thereafter.

FRIANT (FRIE uhnt) **DAM** [Fresno Co.]. Named in 1939. The town of Friant at this site had been named in the 1920s for the lumberman Thomas Friant.

FULLERTON [Orange Co.]. Named in 1887 for George H. Fullerton, president of the land company.

FUNERAL MOUNTAINS [Death Valley N.P.]. Probably so named because they are capped with masses of black rock, which give the impression of mourning.

FURNACE CREEK [Death Valley N.P.]. Named in 1860, probably because of the extremely hot weather.

GABILAN (GAB uh lan) **RANGE** [Monterey, San Benito Cos.]. The name is an alternative spelling for Spanish *gavilán,* "sparrow hawk."

GABRIELINO (gah bree uh LEE noh). Refers to an Indian tribe and their language, which belongs to the Takic branch of the Uto-Aztecan family and, though once spoken in Los Angeles County, is now extinct. This tribe is thought to have been the originators of the religious cult of the god Chingichngich, in which the jimsonweed was consumed as a hallucinogenic drug. The name is Spanish, referring to San Gabriel Mission. The term *Tongva* is now also used to refer to the tribe.

GALLINAS (guh LEE nuhs) [Marin Co.]. Means "hens," from Spanish *gallinas;* the name dates from 1819.

GARBERVILLE [Humboldt Co.]. Named in 1874 for Jacob C. Garber, an early settler.

GARCIA (GAHR see uh, GAHR shuh, gahr SEE uh) RIVER [Mendocino Co.]. Probably named for Rafael García, who had a land grant here in 1844.

GARDENA (gahr DEE nuh) [Los Angeles Co.]. The name was coined from *garden* in the 1880s. **Garden Grove** [Orange Co.] reflects similar motivation.

GARRAPATA (gair uh PAH tuh) CREEK [Monterey Co.]. From the Spanish for "wood tick"; applied in 1835.

GARZAS (GAHR zuhs) CREEK [Stanislaus, Merced Cos.]. From the plural of Spanish *garza,* "heron."

GASQUET (GAS kee) [Del Norte Co.]. Named for the family of Horace Gasquet, an immigrant from France before 1860.

GATO. Spanish for "cat." The term occurs in several place names, referring originally to wildcats; the best known example is **Los Gatos** (GAT uhs) [Santa Clara Co.], "the cats"; there is also a railroad siding called **Gato** [Santa Barbara Co.].

GAVILAN (GAV uh lan) PEAK [Riverside Co.]. From Spanish *gavilán,* "sparrow hawk." An alternative spelling occurs in the name of the **Gabilan Range** [Monterey and San Benito Cos.].

GAVIOTA (gav ee OH tuh) [Santa Barbara Co.]. Spanish for "seagull"; the site was named by Portolá's soldiers in 1769 after they killed a seagull here.

GAZELLE (guh ZEL) [Siskiyou Co.]. The name of a small African antelope was perhaps applied here to distinguish the place from other sites named for the local pronghorn antelope.

GAZOS (GAH zohs, GAZ ohs) **CREEK** [San Mateo, Santa Cruz Cos.]. May be a mangling of Spanish *garzas,* "herons."

GENESEE (JEN uh see) [Plumas Co.]. Also spelled Geneseo, it was named in the 1860s for a place in New York State (where both spellings also occur); the name is of Iroquoian origin.

GILROY (GIL roy) [Santa Clara Co.]. Now famous for the production of garlic, the town was named for the landowner John Gilroy, a Scottish sailor who jumped ship in Monterey in 1815, changed his name to Juan Bautista Gilroy, and became the first non-Spanish permanent settler in California.

GLENDALE [Los Angeles Co.]. The name contains the Celtic word *glen,* meaning a narrow valley; the town was so named around 1891.

GLENDORA [Los Angeles Co.]. A name created in 1887 by George Whitcomb from the word *glen* plus his wife's name, Ledora.

GLENN COUNTY. Founded in 1891 and named for Dr. Hugh J. Glenn, who came to California in 1849, bought Rancho Jacinto in 1867, and became the most important wheat grower in the state. His estate gave financial backing to a proposal for creating and naming the new county.

GODDARD, MOUNT [Kings Canyon N.P.]. Named in 1865 for the civil engineer George H. Goddard, who had contributed much to the knowledge of California geography.

GOETHE (GER tuh), **MOUNT** [Fresno Co.]. Named in 1949 in honor of the German writer and philosopher Johann Wolfgang von Goethe (1749–1832), the author of *Faust*. But **Goethe** (GAY tee) **Grove** in Prairie Creek Redwoods State Park [Humboldt Co.] was named for Charles and Mary Goethe, San Francisco philanthropists.

GOLDEN GATE. The name given by John C. Frémont in 1846 to the entrance of San Francisco Bay, in anticipation not of the Gold Rush, but of the riches of Asia that would enter the port. **Golden Gate National Recreation Area** [San Francisco, Marin Cos.] was established as a federal park in 1972.

GOLETA (goh LEE tuh) [Santa Barbara Co.]. Spanish for "schooner," a type of ship. The name was probably given when a ship was either built or stranded here in the early nineteenth century. Early in World War II, an oil refinery here was shelled by a Japanese submarine.

GONZALES (gahn ZAL uhs) [Monterey Co.]. Named for the landowner Teodoro Gonzales, or for his family. The Spanish surname is also spelled González.

GORDO. Spanish for "fat, plump" (fem. *gorda*); the term has been applied to massive promontories on the coast, such as **Punta Gorda** [Humboldt Co.]—literally, "fat point"—so named in 1775.

GORMAN [Los Angeles Co.]. Named in 1877 for one H. Gorman, the first postmaster.

GRANADA (gruh NAH duh) **HILLS** [Los Angeles Co.]. Named for the onetime Moorish city in Spain. The name occurs elsewhere in California as **El Granada** [San Mateo Co.] and, in an alternate spelling, as **Grenada** [Siskiyou Co.].

GRAPEVINE CANYON [Kern Co.]. A translation of the name given by Pedro Fages in 1772: Cajón de las Uvas, "canyon of the grapes," because of the wild grapevines growing here; it became part of the first direct automobile route between Los Angeles and the Central Valley.

GRASS VALLEY [Nevada Co.]. The name was given to the valley around 1849 because settlers found fodder there for their livestock. The city was so named in 1852.

GRAYBACK [San Bernardino Co.]. Another name for **San Gorgonio Peak.** The word—once a familiar term for the body louse, which often infested pioneer settlers—was sometimes applied to mountains of gray color.

GREENFIELD [Monterey Co.]. Named in 1905, the town is one of many places named with reference to green foliage. However, some places may derive their names from Green as a family name—for example, **Green Creek** [Shasta Co.], named for Myron Green, manager of a fish hatchery.

GREENHORN [Siskiyou Co.]. Named for a greenhorn, or newcomer, during the Gold Rush, who as a joke was sent to look for gold at a site thought to contain no ore—where, of course, he struck it rich.

GRENADA (gruh NAY duh) [Siskiyou Co.]. The name is reminiscent of Granada in Spain, but it may recall Grenada County in Mississippi or Grenada in the West Indies.

GROSSMONT [San Diego Co.]. Named around 1900 for the realtor William B. Gross.

GUADALASCA (gwah duh LAH skuh) [Ventura Co.]. Probably from the Ventureño Chumash village name *shuwalaxsho,* perhaps containing *xsho,* "sycamore." There may have been influence from the *Guad-* of Spanish place names like Guadalajara, reflecting Arabic *wâdi,* "river."

GUADALUPE (gwah duh LOOP, gwah duh LOO pee, gwah duh LOO pay) [Santa Barbara Co.]. Named by the Spanish for Our Lady of Guadalupe, a title given in Mexico to the Virgin Mary. (Guadalupe was originally a place name in Spain, of Arabic origin.) The **Guadalupe River** [Santa Clara Co.] was named even earlier, by a Spanish expedition in 1775.

GUAJOME (wah HOH mee) [San Diego Co.]. From Luiseño *waxáawu-may,* "little frog," the name of an Indian village.

GUALALA (wuh LAH luh) [Sonoma Co.]. From a Kashaya Pomo village name, *walaali,* derived from *ahqha walaali,* "water go-down place." English speakers interpreted this as Walhalla, which in Norse myths was the heavenly home of fallen warriors. In 1862 this name was mistakenly interpreted as Spanish and given the spelling Gualala.

GUASTI (GWAH stee) [San Bernardino Co.]. Named for Secondo Guasti, a leading producer of wines in the area.

GUATAY (gwah TIE) [San Diego Co.]. Probably from Diegueño *wataay,* "big house"—that is, ceremonial house.

GUENOC (GWEN ahk) [Lake Co.]. From the Lake Miwok place name *wénok,* which may in turn be a borrowing from Wappo *wénnokh,* the word used by the Wappo to designate the Southern Pomo tribe.

GUERNEVILLE (GERN vil) [Sonoma Co.]. Named in the 1870s for George E. Guerne, proprietor of a sawmill.

GUILICOS (WIL uh kohs) [Sonoma Co.]. The name given by the Spanish, in the 1820s, to an Indian tribe; the term is from Lake Miwok *wíilok,* "dusty," plus the Spanish masculine plural suffix *-os.*

GUINDA (GWIN duh) [Yolo Co.]. From the Spanish word for the morello, a variety of sour cherry. (The Spanish word is in fact pronounced *GEEN dah.*)

GUSTINE (gus TEEN) [Merced Co.]. Laid out by the land baron Henry Miller around 1900 and named in memory of his daughter Augustine.

HACKAMORE [Modoc Co.]. A western American word for a halter used mainly in breaking horses, from Spanish *jáquima,* "headstall of a bridle."

HAIWEE (HAY way) [Inyo Co.]. From Panamint *heewi,* "dove," or from a related form in some other Numic language.

HAMILTON, MOUNT [Santa Clara Co.]. Named for the Reverend Laurentine Hamilton, one of a party that climbed the peak in 1861.

HANAUPAH (huh NOO pah, HAN uh pah) [Death Valley N.P.]. From the local Panamint Indian language, apparently a combination of *hunuppin,* "canyon," and *paa,* "water."

HANFORD [Kings Co.]. Named in 1877 by the Central Pacific Railway for its treasurer, James Hanford.

HANGTOWN CREEK [El Dorado Co.]. Preserves the nickname of Placerville, called Hangtown during the Gold Rush because some robbers were hanged there in 1849.

The name is preserved in "Hangtown fry," a dish of scrambled eggs, fried oysters, and bacon—said to be a miner's ideal meal.

HARBIN HOT SPRINGS [Lake Co.]. Named for James M. Harbin, who settled here around 1857.

HAT CREEK [Lassen N.P.]. Named in the 1850s, perhaps because a traveler lost his hat in the stream, or perhaps from the Achumawi name for the creek, which is *hatiwïwi.*

HAVASU (HAV uh soo) **LAKE** [San Bernardino Co.]. This artificial lake was named in 1939 from the Mojave word *havasúu,* "blue."

HAVILAH (HAV uh luh) [Kern Co.]. Named in 1864 after a land of gold mentioned in Genesis 2:11.

HAWTHORNE [Los Angeles Co.]. Named about 1906 for the novelist Nathaniel Hawthorne, author of *The Scarlet Letter.*

HAYFORK [Trinity Co.]. The name was first applied to the Hayfork River, regarded as a "fork" of the Trinity River, with reference to local hay fields.

HAYWARD [Alameda Co.]. Named for William Hayward, who opened a hotel here in 1852.

HEALDSBURG [Sonoma Co.]. Named in 1857 for the storekeeper Harmon G. Heald.

HEARST CASTLE [San Luis Obispo Co.]. Built by William Randolph Hearst, publisher of the Hearst newspapers; his father, George Hearst, was a millionaire mining magnate and senator from California in the 1880s.

HECKER PASS [Santa Clara Co.]. Named for Henry Hecker, a county supervisor, when the highway was opened in 1928.

HEDIONDA (hed ee AHN duh) **CREEK** [Santa Clara Co.]. From a Spanish word meaning "stinking," probably applied because of a sulfur spring.

HEMET (HEM uht) [Riverside Co.]. The name dates from 1879 and was formerly also spelled Hemmet. It is probably from Swedish or Danish *hemmet,* "the home." The town is the home of the annual Ramona pageant, recalling the early days of Spanish California.

HERCULES [Contra Costa Co.]. Named for the ancient Greek hero in the 1890s when a gunpowder factory was established there.

HERMOSA (her MOH suh) **BEACH** [Los Angeles Co.]. From the Spanish for "beautiful" (feminine), the name was given by developers in 1901.

HETCH HETCHY (hech HECH ee) **VALLEY** [Yosemite N.P.]. The name was recorded in 1877 as Hatchatchie, probably from Southern Sierra Miwok *aččačča,* "magpie."

HETTEN [Trinity Co.]. From Wintu *xetin,* "camas," an edible root; the name of **Kettenpom Valley** reflects the same word. **Hettenshaw Valley** [Trinity Co.] is from Wintu *xetin č'aaw,* "camas sing"; the plants were said to sing in that location.

HI-CORUM (HIE kor uhm) [San Bernardino Co.]. Named for a Chemehuevi Indian miner who was apparently called *haiku-rïmpa,* "white-man mouth."

HIGHLAND [San Bernardino Co.]. Actually in the lowlands, it was named for the tableland several hundred feet above the valley.

HILLSBOROUGH [San Mateo Co.]. This expensive residential area, incorporated in 1910, is named after Hillsboro, New Hampshire. The smallest building lots here are one-half acre.

HOBO HOT SPRINGS [Kern Co.]. Named in the early 1900s for campers who were disparagingly called hoboes by local farmers.

HOLLISTER [San Benito Co.]. Named in 1868 for W. W. Hollister, who was the first to drive a herd of sheep across the continent and who became owner of San Justo ranch. The name San Justo for the town was rejected by its citizens, who felt there were already too many saints' names in California.

HOLLYWOOD [Los Angeles Co.]. Named in 1886, perhaps for a Hollywood in the eastern United States, or perhaps for Hollywood in County Wicklow, Ireland. The holly bush of the eastern United States does not thrive in southern California; however, the California holly, or toyon, is abundant in the Hollywood hills.

HOLMBY HILLS [Los Angeles Co.]. Named after Holmby, England, birthplace of the landowner Arthur Letts Sr., founder of the Broadway Department Store, Los Angeles.

HOLTVILLE [Imperial Co.]. Named Holton in 1903 by W. F. Holt, president of the Holton Power Company, its name was later changed to its present form.

HOMERS NOSE [Sequoia N.P.]. Jokingly named in 1872 by surveyors because it resembled the nose of Joseph Homer, a member of their party.

HONCUT (HON kuht) [Butte Co.]. From the Maidu Indian village name *hoan'kut.*

HONDO. Spanish for "deep"; the word occurs in many place names. Thus **Rio Hondo** (ree oh HAHN doh) [Los Angeles Co.] means "deep river." The feminine form, **Honda** [Santa Barbara Co.], is the name of a railroad siding.

HONEY LAKE [Lassen Co.]. Supposedly named in 1850 because of a sweet substance deposited by aphids on wild grasses in the area. However, the name may also be from Maidu *hani'lekim,* mentioned in the native creation myth as the name for the lake.

HOOPA VALLEY. *See* Hupa.

HOOSIMBIM (HOO sim bim) **MOUNTAIN** [Trinity Co.]. From Wintu *huusun meem,* literally, "buzzard's water."

HOPLAND [Mendocino Co.]. So named in the 1870s because hops were grown by farmers there as an ingredient for brewing beer.

HORNITOS (hor NEE tuhs) [Mariposa Co.]. The diminutive plural of Spanish *horno,* "oven," the name means "little ovens." It may have been transferred from Los Hornitos in the Mexican state of Durango.

HORSE LINTO (hors LIN tuhn) **CREEK** [Humboldt Co.]. From Hupa *xahslin-ding,* "riffles place," the Indian village originally at the mouth of this creek. The mapmakers' garbled spelling Horse Linto has given rise to the pronunciation *hors LIN toh.*

HUASNA (WAHZ nuh) [San Luis Obispo Co.]. From the Purisimeño Chumash village name *wasna,* of unknown origin.

HUENEME (wie NEE muh, wie NEE mee), **PORT** [Ventura Co.]. From Ventureño Chumash *weneʼmu,* "sleeping place"; so named because it was a stopover for Indians traveling along the coast between Santa Barbara and Point Mugu.

HUERHUERO (wair WAIR oh) **CREEK** and **SODA SPRINGS** [San Luis Obispo Co.]. Possibly from the Obispeño Chumash village name *elewexe,* or from Mexican Spanish *huero,* "rotten," perhaps referring to the odor of sulfur water.

HUMBOLDT BAY. Named in 1850 for the German geographer Alexander von Humboldt, famous for his explorations in South America—who, however, did not visit this area. **Humboldt County** was created in 1853.

HUNTERS POINT [San Francisco Co.]. Named for Robert E. Hunter, who in 1849 participated in a project to found a city here. The area was once famous for its naval shipyard.

HUNTINGTON BEACH [Orange Co.]. Named in 1903 for Henry Huntington, nephew and heir of railroad magnate Collis P. Huntington (he also married his uncle's widow). The younger Huntington was a promoter of electric railroads in southern California and once had the largest land holdings in the region. He was the donor of the Huntington Library and Art Museum in San Marino. His name was also given to **Huntington Park** [Los Angeles Co.].

HUPA (HOO pah). Also spelled Hoopa. Refers to a Humboldt County tribe and their language, of the Athabaskan family. The name is not the tribe's own name for themselves, but was applied by whites; it is derived from *hup'oo,* the name for the **Hoopa Valley** in the language of the neighboring Yurok Indians.

HYAMPOM (HIE uhm pahm) [Trinity Co.]. Probably from Wintu *xayiin-pom,* "slippery place."

IAQUA (IE uh kwah) **BUTTES** [Humboldt Co.]. The name contains a local Indian word of greeting, preserved in the area as Yurok *oyekwi',* Karuk *ayukîi.* It may have meant "friend" in the now extinct Wiyot language.

IBEX PASS [Death Valley N.P.]. Named for the bighorn sheep, locally called ibex—properly the term for the European mountain goat.

IDRIA (ID ree uh) [San Benito Co.]. Named after the New Idria mercury mine, which took its name from Idrija, a source of mercury in Slovenia.

IDYLLWILD (IE duhl wilde) [Riverside Co.]. A name suggested in 1899 as descriptive of the timbered resort area.

IGNACIO (ig NAY shoh) [Marin Co.]. Named for Ignacio Pacheco, grantee of the land here in 1840.

IGO (IE goh) [Shasta Co.]. Probably an Indian name, but associated in folklore with the name of nearby Ono: "I go" and "Oh no!"

IKES FALLS [Humboldt Co.]. Named for a Karuk Indian who lived nearby, called "Little Ike," from his Karuk name, *éehkan*. The term *falls* is used in local English for what might be called rapids elsewhere.

ILLILOUETTE (il il oo ET) **FALL** [Yosemite N.P.]. A garbled representation of Southern Sierra Miwok *ṭiṭilwiyak*, literally, "something shiny." It was earlier recorded as Tulolowehäck and Tooluluwack—as the geologist Josiah Whitney wrote in 1870, "a good illustration of how difficult it is to catch the exact pronunciation of these names."

IMPERIAL VALLEY. The name given in 1901 when the California Development Company planned the settlement of the newly reclaimed desert region. The town of **Imperial** was founded in 1901, and **Imperial County** in 1907.

IÑAJA (IN yuh hah) [San Diego Co.]. From Diegueño *'enyehaa,* "my water" or "my tears."

INAM (i NAHM) [Siskiyou Co.]. From Karuk *inaam,* referring to the site of the world renewal ceremony held each autumn.

INDEPENDENCE [Inyo Co.]. Named after a nearby military base, Camp Independence, established on the Fourth of July in 1862.

INDIA BASIN [San Francisco Co.]. Probably named for cargo ships arriving from India in the nineteenth century.

INDIO (IN dee oh) [Riverside Co.]. Earlier called Indian Wells; in the 1870s the name was changed to the Spanish word for "Indian."

INGLEWOOD [Los Angeles Co.]. Named in 1887 by a visitor from a Canadian town called Inglewood.

IN-KO-PAH (IN koh pah) **MOUNTAIN** [Imperial Co.]. Named by the California Division of Highways on the basis of Diegueño *'enyaak 'iipay,* literally, "east people."

INVERNESS [Marin Co.]. Named in 1899 after the city of Inverness in Scotland.

INYO (IN yoh) **MOUNTAINS**. Named in the 1860s; the term may have an unidentified Indian source, or may be from Spanish *indio,* "Indian." **Inyo County** was named in 1866.

IONE (ie OHN) [Amador Co.]. So named since 1853—perhaps for the town of Ione, Illinois, or for a heroine in a novel by Bulwer-Lytton.

IRVINE (ER vine) [Orange Co.]. Named in 1888 for the landowner James Irvine. The city is said to be the largest master-planned urban community in the United States.

IRVINGTON [Alameda Co.]. Known in the 1870s as Washington Corners; in 1884 it was renamed Irving, perhaps recalling the name of the author Washington Irving. In 1887 the name was further changed to Irvington.

ISABELLA, LAKE [Kern Co.]. The town of Isabella was named in 1893—following the four hundredth anniversary of the voyage of Columbus—in honor of Queen Isabella of Spain. It now lies submerged under the lake.

ISHI PISHI FALLS [Humboldt Co.]. From Karuk *íshipish,* "extending down," referring to a trail that descends from the mountains here.

ISLAIS (IS lis) **CREEK** [San Francisco Co.]. From a plural form of California Spanish *islay*, the hollyleaf cherry bush; the word is borrowed from Salinan *slay'*.

ISLA VISTA (ie luh VIS tuh) [Santa Barbara Co.]. Intended to mean "island view," with reference to the offshore Channel Islands; better Spanish would be *vista de las islas*. The area provides housing for the nearby campus of the University of California at Santa Barbara; it became famous during the Vietnam War when student activists staged demonstrations and burned the local Bank of America building.

IVANHOE [Tulare Co.]. The name was first applied to the school district in 1885, after the novel by Sir Walter Scott.

IVANPAH (IE vuhn pah) [San Bernardino Co.]. From Chemehuevi *avimpa*, "white clay water," from *avi*, "white clay," plus *pa*, "water." It was earlier called Leastalk, an anagram of "Salt Lake."

JACALITOS (jak uh LEE tuhs) **CREEK** [Fresno Co.]. From the plural of Mexican Spanish *jacalito*, "little hut," a diminutive of *jacal*, "hut." The Spanish term is derived in turn from Aztec *xacalli*, "hut."

JACKSON [Amador Co.]. Named around 1850 for "Colonel" Alden M. Jackson, a lawyer from New England. **Jacksonville** [Tuolumne Co.] was also named for him.

JACUMBA (huh KUHM buh, huh KUM buh) [San Diego Co.]. From a Diegueño village name of unknown meaning.

JALAMA (huh LAM uh) [Santa Barbara Co.]. From the Chumash village name *xalam*, meaning "bundle."

JAMACHA (HAM uh shaw) [San Diego Co.]. From Diegueño *hemechaa,* a type of gourd used for soap.

JAMESTOWN [Tuolumne Co.]. Named in 1848 after its founder, George F. James, a San Francisco lawyer. The place is locally known as "Jimtown."

JAMUL (huh MOOL) [San Diego Co.]. From a Diegueño village name, *hemull,* "foam, lather."

JAPACHA (hah puh CHAH) **CREEK** and **PEAK** [San Diego Co.]. The name reflects Diegueño *hapechaa,* "hand stone for grinding," what is called in Spanish *mano de metate.*

JAPATUL (HAH puh tool) [San Diego Co.]. Probably a Diegueño village name, perhaps from *hatepull,* "woodpecker."

JAVON (huh VOHN) **CREEK** [Ventura Co.]. From Spanish *jabón,* "soap," recalling a boom in so-called soap rock found here around 1875. The mineral turned out to be infusorial earth, usable only as a polishing agent, and that was the end of California's "soap bubble."

JAYHAWKER WELL [Death Valley N.P.]. Named for the Jayhawkers, a party of emigrants from Illinois, who camped here in 1849. The term originally referred to antislavery guerrillas who operated in border states during Civil War times.

JEDEDIAH (jed uh DIE uh) **SMITH REDWOODS STATE PARK** [Del Norte Co.]. Named for one of the great explorers of the West, Jedediah Smith (1799–1831); Smith River is also named for him.

JENNY LIND [Calaveras Co.]. Named in the 1850s for the famous Swedish soprano (1820–87), who, however, never visited California.

JIM CROW CREEK [Sierra Co.]. Bears the nickname, given in 1849, of a Kanaka—that is, one of the Hawaiian Islanders who took part in the Gold Rush.

JOBS (JOHBZ) **PEAK** [Alpine Co.]. Named for Moses Job, a storekeeper. An adjacent peak is called **Jobs Sister.**

JOHANNESBURG [Kern Co.]. Named about 1897 after the famous mining center in South Africa. It is popularly known as "Joburg."

JOLON (huh LOHN) [Monterey Co.]. From Salinan *xolon,* "it leaks, a leak; a channel where water cuts through." Local folklore claims that the name originated when bandits would stop stagecoaches by shouting, "Hol' on! Hol' on!"

JONATA (hoh NAH tuh, HAH nuh tuh) [Santa Barbara Co.]. A simplification of Spanish Jonjonata, from Chumash *xonxon'ata,* "tall oak."

JOSHUA TREE NATIONAL MONUMENT [Riverside, San Bernardino Cos.]. Named for the distinctive desert tree, a variety of yucca. The tree was so called by Mormon emigrants during the Gold Rush, to whom it seemed to be a symbol of Joshua leading them to the promised land.

JUANEÑO (hwah NAYN yoh). Refers to a tribe living in Orange County and to their language, which belongs to the Takic branch of the Uto-Aztecan family. The name is Spanish, referring to San Juan Capistrano Mission. Currently the native name Ajachmem is also used in referring to the tribe.

JUAQUAPIN (wah kwuh PEEN) **CREEK** [San Diego Co.]. Perhaps from Diegueño *hakupin,* "warm water."

JUNIPERO (huh NIP er oh) **SERRA PEAK** [Monterey Co.]. Named for Padre Junípero Serra (1713–84), founder of the first nine missions in Alta California.

JURUPA (huh ROO puh) **MOUNTAINS** [Riverside, San Bernardino Cos.]. From Gabrielino *horúv-nga*, "sage-brush place," or a similar form in a related language.

KAISER CREEK and **PEAK** [Fresno Co.]. Named as early as 1862, perhaps for Elijah Keyser, a gold miner from Pennsylvania.

KALMIA (kal MEE uh) **LAKE** [Trinity Co.]. Named for a shrub, the American laurel or alpine laurel (*Kalmia polifolia*), which grows here. The Latin genus name of the plant, from the name of the eighteenth-century Finnish botanist Peter Kalm, is usually pronounced by botanists as *KAL mee uh.*

KANGAROO MOUNTAIN [Siskiyou Co.]. Probably named not for the Australian marsupial, but for the kangaroo rat native to California.

KARUK (KAH rook). Formerly also spelled Karok, the term refers to an Indian tribe and language of Humboldt and Siskiyou Counties; the tribal headquarters are at Happy Camp. The name of the tribe is from the word *káruk,* "upriver," contrasting with *yúruk,* "downriver"; the latter was the term applied by whites to the Yurok tribe of the lower Klamath.

KASHIA (kuh SHIE uh). Refers to an Indian tribe, also called Southwest Pomo, of Sonoma County and their language, which belongs to the Pomo family. The term comes from their name for themselves, *k'ahšáaya,* "agile people."

KATIMIN (KAH tee meen) [Siskiyou Co.]. From Karuk *ka'tim'iin,* literally, "upper-edge falls," referring to a major rapids in the Klamath River and to the adjacent Indian village.

KATO. *See* Cahto.

KAWAIISU (kah WIE uh soo). Refers to an Indian tribe in Kern County and their language, which belongs to the Numic branch of the Uto-Aztecan family. The term is the name applied to them by the neighboring Yokuts Indians.

KAWEAH (kuh WEE ah) **RIVER** [Sequoia N.P.]. Named for the Yokuts tribe *kawia* or *gáwia*. The name has no relation to that of the Cahuilla Indians in Riverside County, although it is similarly pronounced.

KEARSARGE (KEER sahrj) **PEAK** [Inyo Co.]. Named by Union sympathizers during the Civil War, when the Union man-of-war *Kearsarge* destroyed the Confederate ship *Alabama*. The Union warship was named after Mount Kearsarge in New Hampshire. The name of that mountain is from an Abenaki (Algonquian) word meaning "high place."

KEKAWAKA (KIK uh wah kuh) **CREEK** [Trinity Co.]. From Wintu *kiki waqat*, "frozen creek."

KELSEYVILLE [Lake Co.]. Named for Andrew Kelsey, the first settler in the county, killed in 1849 by Indians because of his mistreatment of them.

KELUCHE (kuh LOO chee) **CREEK** [Shasta Co.]. Named after Charlie Klutchie or Keluche, a Wintu shaman; his Wintu name was *tl'učuheres*, from *tl'uči*, "sticking, stabbing."

KENTFIELD [Marin Co.]. Named in 1905 for Albert Emmett Kent, an early settler.

KERN RIVER [Kern Co.]. Named in 1845 by the explorer John C. Frémont, in honor of Edward M. Kern, his topographer, who nearly drowned in these notoriously rough waters. **Kern County** was named in 1866; and the town of Whiskey Flat was renamed **Kernville** in the same period.

KETTENPOM VALLEY (KET uhn pahm) [Trinity Co.]. From Wintu *xetin-pom,* "camas place," from *xetin,* "camas," an edible bulb. *See also* Hetten.

KETTLEMAN HILLS [Kings Co.]. Named in the 1890s for David Kettleman, a forty-niner and cattleman. **Kettleman City** was founded in 1919.

KIAVAH (KIE uh vah) **MOUNTAIN** [Kern Co.]. Named in 1906 for a Panamint Indian who moved to the area.

KIBESILLAH (kib uh SIL uh) [Mendocino Co.]. Northern Pomo for "flat rock": *khabé,* "rock," plus *silá,* "flat."

KIMSHEW (KIM shoo) **CREEK** [Butte Co.]. The name is from Konkow (Northwestern Maidu) *kiwim sewi,* "the stream on the other side," referring to the North Fork of the Feather River.

KING CITY [Monterey Co.]. Named for the landowner Charles Henry King.

KINGS RIVER. Named Río de los Santos Reyes, "river of the Holy Kings" (i.e., the three Magi), by a party of Spanish explorers in 1805; the English name came to be applied in the 1850s. **Kings County** was formed in 1893; **Kings Canyon National Park** was created in 1940.

KIT CARSON PASS [Alpine Co.]. Named for the frontiersman Christopher "Kit" Carson (1809–68).

KITTINELBE (kit uh NEL bee) [Humboldt Co.]. From Wintu *xetin-elba,* "eating camas" (an edible bulb), although the site is in the territory of neighboring Athabaskan tribes. It is now also called Phillipsville.

KLAMATH (KLAM uhth) **RIVER** [Siskiyou, Humboldt, Del Norte Cos.]. From *tlamatl,* the Chinook name for the Klamath tribe, which lives around Klamath Lake in Oregon—the source of the river. The town of **Klamath** [Del Norte Co.] takes its name from the river.

KOIP PEAK [Yosemite N.P.]. From Northern Paiute *kóipa* or Mono *koippï,* "mountain sheep."

KOKOWEEP (koh koh WEEP) **PEAK** [San Bernardino Co.]. May be from Southern Paiute *kogo,* "gopher snake," plus *uippi,* "canyon."

KONKOW. *See* Concow.

KONOCTI (kuh NAHK tie), **MOUNT** [Lake Co.]. Supposedly from Pomo *kno'ktai,* derived from *kno,* "mountain," and *xatai,* "woman."

KUNA (KOO nuh) **PEAK** [Yosemite N.P.]. Takes its name from *kúna,* the word for "fire" in several Numic languages of eastern California, including Southern Paiute, Chemehuevi, and Kawaiisu.

KYBURZ (KIE berz) [El Dorado Co.]. Named in 1911 for the first postmaster, Albert Kyburz.

LA BREA (luh BRAY uh) **TAR PITS** [Los Angeles Co.]. The Spanish name means "the tar"; hence the common phrase "the La Brea Tar Pits" is doubly redundant.

LA CAÑADA [Los Angeles Co.]. The Spanish word *cañada,* "valley," occurring in many place names, is often spelled in English simply as Canada and is pronounced variously as *KAN uh duh, kuh NAH duh, kuhn YAD uh,* and *kuhn YAH duh.* The best-known example is La Cañada, whose name, after a merger in 1979 with the settlement of Flintridge, officially became **La Cañada Flintridge.**

LA CRESCENTA (kruh SEN tuh) [Los Angeles Co.]. *Not* Spanish for "the crescent," which would be *la creciente*. The artificial name was given in the early 1880s by Dr. Benjamin B. Briggs, who said he could see three crescent-shaped land formations from his home.

LAFAYETTE [Contra Costa Co.]. Named in 1853 for the Marquis de Lafayette, the French general who fought for American independence.

LA GRANGE [Stanislaus Co.]. French for "the farm." La Grange was the name of the Marquis de Lafayette's country home in France; it thus became popular as a U.S. place name.

LAGUNA (luh GOO nuh). Used in California Spanish to mean "lake," the word is found in many place names— often in combinations, like **Laguna Seca** (SAY kuh) [Santa Clara Co.], meaning "dry lake"; **Laguna Honda** (HAHN duh) [San Francisco Co.], "deep lake"; and **Laguna Salada** (suh LAH duh) [San Mateo Co.], "salty lake." The name of **Laguna Canyon** [Orange Co.] has been known since 1841; the town of **Laguna Beach** was named after the canyon. **Laguna Niguel** (ni GEL), in the same area, is from the name of an Indian site that the Spanish called Nigüili, Nigüel, or Neuil, from Juaneño *nawíl*. **Lagunitas** (lah guh NEE tuhs) [Marin Co.] means "little lakes."

LA HABRA (HAH bruh) [Orange Co.]. Corresponds to standard Spanish *abra*, "a gorge, a pass through the mountains"; although it is feminine, standard Spanish nouns beginning with accented *a* take the article *el*, so one would expect *el (h)abra*. The term refers here to the pass through the Puente Hills traversed by the Portolá expedition in 1769.

LA HONDA (HON duh) **CREEK** [San Mateo Co.]. Known in the 1830s as Arroyo Hondo, "deep creek"; after 1857 it was misspelled Arroyo Honda, and later it was given its present form. The settlement of **La Honda** was named for the creek around 1880.

LA JOLLA (HOY yuh) [San Diego Co.]. *Hoya,* also spelled *joya* or *jolla,* is a common Mexican Spanish geographical term for "hollow." There is no evidence that the site was named from Spanish *la joya,* "the jewel." However, an alternative etymology is from Diegueño *mat-ku-laahuuy,* "place that has holes or caves," related to *llehup,* "hole."

LAKE COUNTY. Created in 1861, it was named after Clear Lake.

LAKE MERCED (mer SED) [San Francisco Co.]. Named in 1775 in honor of Nuestra Señora de la Merced, "Our Lady of Mercy."

LAMANDA PARK [Los Angeles Co.]. The name was coined in 1886 by Leonard Rose, who added the *L* from his own name to his wife's given name, Amanda.

LA MESA [San Diego Co.]. Spanish for "the table(-land)"; it was first named La Mesa Heights in 1886.

LA MIRADA (muh RAH duh) [Los Angeles Co.]. Spanish for "the glance, the gaze"; the name was given in 1888.

LANCHA PLANA (lahn chuh PLAH nuh) [Calaveras Co.]. Spanish for "flat boat," in reference to a ferry used here in the 1850s.

LA PANZA (PAHN zuh) [San Luis Obispo Co.]. Spanish for "the paunch," referring to the practice of using a beef stomach as bait for catching bears in the 1820s.

LA POSTA (POH stuh) [San Diego Co.]. Spanish for "the relay stage or post," where mail riders used to stop.

LA PUENTE (poo EN tee, PWEN tee) [Los Angeles Co.]. Spanish for "the bridge." In modern standard Spanish, the word is masculine, hence *el puente.* The place is also called simply Puente.

LAS CRUCES (KROO suhs) [Santa Barbara Co.]. Spanish for "the crosses"; the name was given to a land grant in 1836.

LAS FLORES (FLOR uhs) [San Diego Co.]. Spanish for "the flowers," the abundance of which was noted here in 1769.

LAS GARZAS (GAHR zuhs) **CREEK** [Monterey Co.]. Spanish for "the herons."

LAS LLAJAS (YAH huhs) **CANYON** [Ventura Co.]. Probably a misspelling of Spanish *las llagas,* "the wounds," referring to the stigmata of a saint.

LASSEN PEAK [Plumas Co.]. Also called Mount Lassen, it was named in the 1850s for Peter Lassen, a pioneer settler from Denmark. He was murdered in 1859 while seeking a silver mine. **Lassen County** was created in 1864, and **Lassen Volcanic National Park** in 1916.

LASSIC (LAS ik). The name of an Indian tribe of the Athabaskan family and their language, once spoken in Humboldt County. The term was supposedly the name of their last chief; however, his name was probably from the neighboring Wintu language, in which *lasik* means "bag." The term was applied to **Mount Lassic** [Trinity Co.]; other mountains nearby are called **Black Lassic Peak** and **Red Lassic Peak.**

LAS TRAMPAS (TRAHM puhs) **CREEK** [Contra Costa Co.]. Spanish for "the traps," referring to snares set to catch elk in early times.

LAS TRANCAS (TRANG kuhs) **CREEK** [San Mateo, Santa Cruz Cos.]. The name is Spanish for "the barriers," often referring to cattle guards.

LASUEN (lah soo AYN), **POINT** [Los Angeles Co.]. Named in 1792 for Padre Fermín Francisco de Lasuén, whose name also occurs in Point Fermin.

LAS VIRGENES (VER juh nuhs) **CREEK** [Ventura, Los Angeles Cos.]. Spanish for "the virgins"; it was given in 1802, referring to the virgin martyrs of the church calendar.

LAVA BEDS NATIONAL MONUMENT [Modoc, Siskiyou Cos.]. Created in 1925. The volcanic formations became well known during the Modoc War of 1872–73, in which the Indians used them as strongholds.

LA VERNE [Los Angeles Co.]. Named in 1916 after the promoter of the subdivision, whose given name was La Verne.

LAVIGIA (lah VIG ee uh) **HILL** [Santa Barbara Co.]. Spanish for "the lookout"; the hill was so named in 1828.

LEBEC (luh BEK) [Kern Co.]. Named for Peter Lebeck, who was killed here by a grizzly bear in 1837.

LECHUSA (luh CHOO suh) **CANYON** [Los Angeles Co.]. *Lechuza* is Spanish for "barn owl"; the name was applied in Spanish times.

LEE VINING (lee VIE ning, luh VIE ning) [Mono Co.]. Named for Lee (Leroy) Vining, a settler here in the 1860s.

LEHAMITE (luh HAH muh tee) **FALLS** [Yosemite N.P.]. Probably from Southern Sierra Miwok *leeha'-mite,* "there are several syringa bushes," from *leeha,* "syringa, mock orange, arrowwood."

LEMOORE (luh MOOR) [Kings Co.]. Named in 1875 for Dr. Lovern Lee Moore, an early settler.

LENNOX [Los Angeles Co.]. Named sometime before 1921 after Lenox, Massachusetts.

LEUCADIA (loo KAY dee uh) [San Diego Co.]. Named in 1885 for one of the Ionian Islands in Greece, from whose cliffs the poet Sappho is said to have leaped into the sea. The word is derived from Greek *leukós,* "white."

LIEBRE (lee AY bree) **MOUNTAIN** [Los Angeles Co.]. From the Spanish word for "jackrabbit," applied here in 1825.

LIKELY [Modoc Co.]. Supposedly so named in 1878 when several suggested names had been rejected by the Post Office Department, and it was thought not "likely" that an acceptable name could be found.

LILAC [San Diego Co.]. Named for the California lilac, or ceanothus, a flowering bush unrelated to the domestic lilac.

LINDA [Yuba Co.]. Named in 1850 for a steamship. Apart from being a girl's name, the word is Spanish for "pretty," feminine of *lindo.* **Linda Vista** [San Diego Co.], named in 1886, means "pretty view."

LINDSAY [Tulare Co.]. The name was given in 1888 by the settlement's founder, Captain A. J. Hutchinson; it was his wife's maiden name.

LINGO CANYON [San Luis Obispo Co.]. Named for George Lingo, an early settler.

LISQUE (LEE skay) **CREEK** [Santa Barbara Co.]. Probably from a Spanish spelling, Lisgüey, for the Chumash village name *aliswey,* "in the tarweed."

LIVERMORE [Alameda Co.]. Named for Robert Livermore, an English sailor who jumped ship in 1822, became a Mexican citizen, and obtained the vast land grant that became known as the Livermore Valley.

LLAGAS (YAY guhs, YAH guhs) **CREEK** [Santa Clara Co.]. Takes its name from a site called Las Llagas de Nuestro Padre San Francisco, "the wounds (stigmata) of Our Father Saint Francis," in 1774.

LLANADA (yuh NAH duh) [San Benito Co.]. Spanish for "plain; level ground."

LLANO (YAH noh) [Los Angeles Co.]. Also Spanish for "plain."

LOBITOS (loh BEE tuhs) [San Mateo Co.]. Spanish for "little wolves," *lobitos* is the diminutive plural of *lobo,* "wolf," which refers in California Spanish to the *lobo marino,* "sea wolf"—that is, the marine mammal we call a sea lion in English. **Point Lobos** [Monterey Co.] was named for its numerous sea lions in 1770.

LOCH LOMOND (lahk LOH muhnd) [Santa Cruz Co.]. Named for the famous lake in Scotland.

LOCONOMA (loh kuh NOH muh) **VALLEY** [Lake Co.]. From Wappo *lóknoma,* "goose place."

LODI (LOH die) [San Joaquin Co.]. Named for a town in Italy, the scene of Napoleon's first spectacular victory in 1796.

LODOGA (luh DOH guh) [Colusa Co.]. Also spelled Ladoga, it may have been named after towns in Indiana or Wisconsin, or after the large lake near St. Petersburg in Russia.

LOKOYA (luh KOY uh) [Napa Co.]. May be abbreviated from Locoallomi, the name of a land grant dated 1841. It is probably from Lake Miwok *lakáh-yomi,* "cottonwood place," or *lakáa-yomi,* "goose place."

LOLA, MOUNT [Nevada Co.]. Named for the actress Lola Montez, famous for her liaisons with rich and powerful men such as the King of Bavaria; in 1848 she precipitated a revolution in Munich. She eventually settled in Grass Valley, where she made the child actress Lotta Crabtree her protegée and kept a pet bear.

LOLETA (loh LEE tuh) [Humboldt Co.]. Residents in 1893 sought a name from the local Wiyot Indian language. An elderly Indian jokingly told them that the site was called *hóš wiwítak,* "let's have sex!"—the latter part of which was garbled as Loleta.

LOMA (LOH muh). The Spanish term means "hill" and has been used in many combinations: **Loma Alta** (AHL tuh) [Marin Co.], meaning "high hill"; **Loma Pelona** (puh LOH nuh) [San Luis Obispo Co.], "bald hill"; and **Loma Verde** (VER dee) [Los Angeles Co.], "green hill." **Loma Prieta** (pree ET uh, pree AY tuh) [Santa Clara Co.], "dark hill," a triangulation station of the U.S. Geological Survey, became famous in 1989 as the center of the major earthquake that ruptured the San Francisco Bay Bridge and a freeway in Oakland. **Loma Linda** [San Bernardino Co.] is Spanish for "pretty hill"; the name was applied in 1901. **Point Loma** [San Diego Co.] stands for Punta de la Loma, "point of the hill," the name applied in 1782.

LOMITA (loh MEE tuh) [Los Angeles Co.]. Spanish for "little hill," *lomita* is the diminutive of *loma.*

LOMPOC (LAWM pohk, LOHM pahk) [Santa Barbara Co.]. From the Chumash place name *lompo', olompo',* perhaps meaning "stagnant water." The town was originally a temperance community but later was featured in many films of the bibulous comedian W. C. Fields.

LONG BEACH [Los Angeles Co.]. Named in 1882 with this descriptive term. But **Long Lake** [Plumas Co.] was probably named for someone with the surname Long, since the lake itself is not long.

LOS ALAMOS (AL uh mohs) [Santa Barbara Co.]. Means "the poplars (or cottonwoods)," from Spanish *álamo,* "poplar (or cottonwood)."

LOS ALTOS (AL tohs) [Santa Clara Co.]. Spanish for "the heights," applied here in 1907.

LOS ANGELES (AN juh luhs, ANG guh luhs). Founded on the site of a Gabrielino Indian village called Yangna, or more accurately *iyáanga',* "poison-oak place." The Portolá expedition camped here in 1769, on a stream that they named for Nuestra Señora de los Ángeles de Porciúncula, "Our Lady of the Angels of Porciuncula"—referring to the chapel where the Franciscan order was founded, near Assisi, Italy. In 1779 the name Reina de los Ángeles, "Queen of the Angels," was given to the Spanish settlement, but it came to be known commonly as the Pueblo de Los Angeles. The present abbreviated version was established when **Los Angeles County** was organized and the city incorporated in 1850.

LOS BANOS (BAN uhs) [Merced Co.]. From Spanish *los baños,* "the baths," a term used in the 1840s to refer to pools near the source of **Los Banos Creek.**

LOS BERROS (BAIR ohs) **CREEK** [San Luis Obispo Co.]. The Spanish term means "the watercress."

LOS COCHES (KOH chuhs) **MOUNTAIN** [Santa Barbara Co.]. From a Spanish phrase meaning "the pigs," plural of Mexican Spanish *cochi, coche,* "pig"—unrelated to *coche,* "coach, car, automobile."

LOS FELIZ (FEE lis, fuh LEES) [Los Angeles Co.]. The name of an 1843 land grant, it means "the Feliz family," referring to the heirs of José Féliz (also spelled Félis and Félix), who settled near here in 1813.

LOS GATOS (GAT uhs) [Santa Clara Co.]. Spanish for "the cats," originally referring to wildcats.

LOS MEDANOS (muh DAH nohs) [Contra Costa Co.]. Derived, with a shift of accent, from Spanish *los médanos* (or *méganos*), "the sand dunes," a name given in 1817.

LOS NIETOS (nee ET ohs) [Los Angeles Co.]. The name of a 1797 land grant, it means "the Nieto family," referring to the heirs of Manuel Nieto, the original grantee.

LOS OLIVOS (uh LEE vohs) [Santa Barbara Co.]. Spanish for "the olive trees," applied here around 1890.

LOS PADRES NATIONAL FOREST [Monterey, San Luis Obispo, Santa Barbara, Ventura Cos.]. Named in 1936 to commemorate the Franciscan padres who founded the California missions.

LOSPE (LOHS pay) **MOUNTAIN** [Santa Barbara Co.]. From Chumash *lospe,* "flower."

LOS PENASQUITOS (pen uh SKEE tohs) **CREEK** [San Diego Co.]. The name *peñasquitos,* "small crags," was given in 1823.

LOST HILLS [Kern Co.]. Refers to slight elevations that seem to belong to the Kettleman Hills but look as if they were "lost."

LUCERNE (loo SERN, luh SERN) [Lake Co.]. Named for a city in Switzerland. However, **Lucerne Valley** [Kings Co.] was named in 1912 for *lucerne,* an old term for alfalfa.

LUCIA (loo SEE uh) [Monterey Co.]. The post office, no longer in use, was established about 1900 and was so named because the settlement is at the foot of the Santa Lucia Mountains.

LUISEÑO (loo uh SAYN yoh). Refers to a tribe and their language, which belongs to the Takic branch of the Uto-Aztecan family and is spoken in Riverside and San Diego

Counties. The term is Spanish, referring to San Luis Rey Mission.

LYELL (LIE uhl), **MOUNT** [Yosemite N.P.]. Named in 1863 for the English geologist Charles Lyell.

LYNWOOD [Los Angeles Co.]. Named for Lynn Wood Sessions, the wife of a dairy owner in the area.

MAACAMA (may AK uh muh) **CREEK** [Sonoma Co.]. Named for the Wappo village of *maiya'kma; see also* Mayacmas Mountains.

MACHESNA (muh CHES nuh) **MOUNTAIN** [San Luis Obispo Co.]. Apparently a Spanish version of the name of the McChesney family, early settlers of the area.

MADERA (muh DAIR uh). Spanish for "wood," the name was applied when the new lumber town was founded in 1876. **Madera County** was formed in 1893 and named after the town.

MAD RIVER [Humboldt, Trinity Cos.]. Named in 1849 by members of an exploring party led by Dr. Josiah Gregg, who got "mad" at his companions when they refused to wait for him as he tried to determine the latitude of the river mouth.

MADRONE (muh DROHN) [Santa Clara Co.]. This name of a native tree (*Arbutus menziesii*) with attractive red peeling bark is derived from Spanish *madroño.* According to a Karuk myth, the madrone was once a young man who had an illegitimate love affair; his skin peeled off in shame as he was transformed into a tree.

MAGALIA (muh GAIL yuh) [Butte Co.]. A Latin word for "cottages."

MAHALA (muh HAH luh) **CREEK** [Humboldt Co.]. The term *mahala* was once used in California English to mean "Indian woman"; it may be a corruption of Spanish *mujer*, "woman," or it may come from a Yokuts term such as Chowchilla *mokheelo*, "woman."

MAIDU (MIE doo). A cover term for a group of related Indian tribes and languages found in Butte, Plumas, Yuba, Sierra, Nevada, Placer, Sacramento, and El Dorado Counties. The name is derived from the word for "human being" in the Maidu languages. Subgroups include those called Concow and Nisenan.

MALAGA (MAL uh guh) [Fresno Co.]. Named around 1885 for the malaga grape, which takes its name in turn from the city of Málaga in Spain.

MALIBU (MAL uh boo) [Los Angeles Co.]. From the Chumash village name, spelled Umalibu by the Spanish. The original form may have been *(hu-)mal-iwu,* "it makes a loud noise all the time over there," referring to the surf.

MALPASO (mal PAS oh) **CREEK** [Monterey Co.]. From Spanish *mal paso,* "bad passage," referring to a place where it is difficult to travel.

MAMMOTH MOUNTAIN, LAKES, and **CREEK** [Mono Co.]. Named for the Mammoth Mining Company, which flourished here around 1878; the name was intended to suggest great size, like that of the prehistoric elephant called the mammoth.

MAN EATEN LAKE [Siskiyou Co.]. The lake, which the Karuk call *ára u'ipamvâanatihirak,* "the place where a person ate himself long ago," is the setting for a legend about a man who, in a fit of cannibalism, ate his entire family and finally devoured his own flesh; at the end he became a roving skeleton, still seeking food.

MANGALAR (mang guh LAHR) SPRING [San Diego Co.]. From Mexican Spanish *manglar*, "place of the sumac," from *mangle*, "sumac."

MANHATTAN BEACH [Los Angeles Co.]. Named in 1902 after New York's Manhattan Island, whose name was originally Algonquian.

MANRESA (man REE suh) [Santa Cruz Co.]. Once the site of Villa Manresa, a Roman Catholic retreat named after Manresa, Spain, a site associated with Saint Ignatius Loyola.

MANTECA (man TEE kuh) [San Joaquin Co.]. Spanish for "butter" or "lard"; the town was so named because of a local creamery.

MANZANAR (man zuh NAHR) [Inyo Co.]. Spanish for "apple orchard" (from *manzana*, "apple"). The site is known for a relocation camp in which Japanese Americans were interned during World War II.

MANZANITA (man zuh NEE tuh) [San Diego Co.]. Refers to a native shrub, genus *Arctostaphylos;* the Spanish name, meaning "little apple" (from *manzana*, "apple"), was applied because of its berries.

MARE ISLAND [Solano Co.]. A translation from Spanish Isla de la Yegua, "isle of the mare," supposedly named around 1840 after a mare belonging to General Mariano G. Vallejo.

MARICOPA (mair uh KOH puh) [Kern Co.]. Named in 1904 for an Indian tribe of Arizona, originally called Cocomaricopa (a name of unknown origin).

MARIN (muh RIN). The name was originally applied around 1830 to what are now called the **Marin Islands,**

between San Pedro and San Quentin Points, perhaps because the bay there was named Bahía de Nuestra Señora del Rosario la Marinera, "bay of Our Lady of the Rosary, she of seafarers." It is also possible that the name was that of a local Indian named Marin. Later the name was applied to the **Marin Peninsula** and to **Marin County.**

MARINA (muh REE nuh) [Monterey Co.]. Spanish for "shore, seacoast," now widely used to designate a small-boat harbor. **Marina del Rey** (del RAY) [Los Angeles Co.] is literally "seacoast of the king," but the name comes from adjacent Playa del Rey, "beach of the king."

MARIPOSA (mair uh POH zuh, mair uh POH suh) CREEK [Mariposa Co.]. Named in 1806 with the Spanish word for "butterfly" because the Spanish encountered multitudes of butterflies in this area. The town of **Mariposa** was founded in 1849, and **Mariposa County** in 1850. The native flower called the mariposa lily (*Calochortus* spp.) takes its name from the California toponym.

MARKLEEVILLE [Alpine Co.]. Named in 1863 for Jacob J. Marklee, an early settler who was later killed in a quarrel over the town site.

MARTINEZ (mahr TEE nuhs) [Contra Costa Co.]. Named in 1849 for the landowner Ignacio Martínez, who had been *comandante* at the Presidio of San Francisco from 1822 to 1827.

MAR VISTA [Los Angeles Co.]. The name, given in 1904, is pseudo-Spanish, suggesting "view of the sea" (not "spoil the view"; more grammatical would be Vista del Mar).

MARYSVILLE [Yuba Co.]. Named around 1850 for Mary Murphy Covillaud, the wife of the landowner Charles Covillaud.

MATAGUAL (mah tuh WAHL) **VALLEY** [San Diego Co.]. Named for a Diegueño village known since 1795. The Diegueño name may have been *mak aahway,* "place kill" (i.e., battleground), or *mat-iihway,* "ground red," related to *'ehwatt,* "red."

MATHLES (MATH luhs) **CREEK** [Shasta Co.]. Probably from Wintu *maałas,* "baked salmon."

MATILIJA (muh TIL uh hah) [Ventura Co.]. The name of a Chumash village; its original meaning is unknown. The matilija poppy (*Romneya trichocalyx*) takes its name from this place.

MATILTON (muh TIL tuhn) [Humboldt Co.]. This former village site of the Hupa (Athabaskan) Indians, also called Captain John's Ranch, bears the Hupa name *me'dil-ding,* "canoe place."

MATTOLE (muh TOHL). Refers to an Athabaskan Indian tribe and language of Humboldt County; the people called themselves *bedool,* and the neighboring Wiyot called them *me'tuul.* The name of the tribe was given to the modern town of **Mattole** and to the **Mattole River**.

MATURANGO (mat uh RANG goh) **PEAK** [Inyo Co.]. Perhaps from Spanish *maturrango,* "bad horseman; clumsy, rough person"; or from a Panamint form such as *mat-tootoongwïni,* "stand braced, as against the wind"; or from Panamint *muatangga,* the name for Koso Hot Springs.

MAYACMAS (may YAK muhs, muh YAK muhs) **MOUN-TAINS** [Sonoma, Lake Cos.]. The name is derived from a Wappo village called *maiya'kma;* the original meaning of the name is not known. *See also* Maacama.

MCCLOUD (muh KLOWD) **RIVER** [Siskiyou, Shasta Cos.]. Originally named for Alexander R. McLeod of the Hudson's Bay Company, who trapped in California in

1828–29. After 1855 the name became associated with the early settler Ross McCloud.

MCKINLEYVILLE [Humboldt Co.]. Named in honor of President William McKinley after his assassination in 1901.

MELONES (muh LOH neez) [Calaveras Co.]. Named after a hill and a gold mine called in Spanish Melones, "melons," for unknown reasons.

MENDOCINO (men duh SEE noh), **CAPE** [Humboldt Co.]. The name is recorded from 1587; it is a Spanish adjective derived from the surname Mendoza, referring to one of two viceroys of Mexico who bore that surname. **Mendocino County** was so named in 1850, although the cape has never been in the county. The town of **Mendocino** was named around 1852.

MENDOTA (men DOH tuh) [Fresno Co.]. Named in 1895, probably for a town in Wisconsin or one in Minnesota. The name is originally Siouan, perhaps referring to the confluence of two streams.

MENLO PARK [San Mateo Co.]. Named in 1854 for Menlough, County Galway, Ireland. The town so called in New Jersey, associated with Thomas A. Edison, was named for the one in California.

MERCED (mer SED) **RIVER** [Merced Co.]. Named in 1896 after Nuestra Señora de la Merced, "Our Lady of Mercy." **Merced County** was established with this name in 1855, and the city of **Merced** in 1872.

MERRITT, LAKE [Alameda Co.]. Named in 1891 for Dr. Samuel J. Merritt, mayor of Oakland in 1869.

MESA (MAY suh). The Spanish word for "table," referring to a plateaulike hill, occurs in many California place names such as **La Mesa** [San Diego Co.]. The name of

Mesa Grande [San Diego Co.] means "large table (-land)."

MESCAL (mes KAL). The Mexican Spanish term, from Aztec *mexcalli,* refers to several desert plants, the stems and leaves of which were roasted and eaten by California Indians. The **Mescal Range** [San Bernardino Co.] was named after *Yucca mojavensis* in particular.

MESCALITAN (mes KAL uh tuhn) ISLAND [Santa Barbara Co.]. The name given by the Spanish in 1769 was Mescaltitlán, probably after a town in Mexico. The original meaning is "among the mescal plants." The abbreviated form **Mescal Island** is also used.

MESQUITE (mes KEET). The common name for a desert tree, genus *Prosopis;* the word is from Aztec *mizquitl.* It occurs in several desert place names such as **Mesquite Springs** [Death Valley N.P.] and **Mesquite Dry Lake** [San Bernardino Co.]. The plant bears a nutritious bean, often eaten by desert Indians.

MIAMI MOUNTAIN [Mariposa Co.]. The name is perhaps the local Indian (Yokuts) name *Me-ah-nee.* Association with the eastern place name Miami, itself of Indian origin, may account for the current form.

MILL VALLEY [Marin Co.]. Named in 1889 for a sawmill that was established here in 1834—the one that also gave its name to nearby Corte Madera ("sawmill").

MILPITAS (mil PEE tuhs) [Santa Clara Co.]. The word is Mexican Spanish for "little cornfields," from *milpa,* "cornfield," derived from Aztec *milpan,* "in the field."

MINERAL KING [Tulare Co.]. Originally the name of a mining area, proclaimed "the king of mineral districts." The scenic valley was surveyed by the Disney

Corporation for a ski resort in the 1960s but was saved by the efforts of conservationists; in 1978 it became part of Sequoia National Park.

MIRAMAR (MEER uh mahr) [San Diego Co.]. Corresponds to Spanish *mira el mar,* "looks at the sea," referring to the ocean view; it is now known for its naval air station.

MIRAMONTES (meer uh MOHN tuhs) **POINT** [San Mateo Co.]. Named for a Miramontes family who settled near here in 1840. The place name has been misinterpreted as meaning "mountain view."

MISSION SAN JOSE (san hoh ZAY, san oh ZAY) [Alameda Co.]. The site of the original mission after which the city and county of San Jose were later named. In Spanish times, the city of San Jose was the center of civil government, whereas the mission held religious jurisdiction.

MISSION VIEJO (vee AY hoh) [Orange Co.]. Appears to mean "old mission," but there is a gender error: The Spanish would be *misión vieja.* In fact, the community founded in the 1960s takes its name from Rancho Misión Viejo, a land grant of 1845, meaning "the old ranch [of the] mission" (referring to Mission San Juan Capistrano).

MIWOK (MEE wahk, MEE wuhk). A cover term for a group of related tribes and languages, spoken in several areas: Coast Miwok in Marin County, Lake Miwok in Lake County, Bay Miwok (Saclan) in Contra Costa County, Plains Miwok in San Joaquin County, and several Sierra Miwok groups in Amador, Calaveras, Tuolumne, and Mariposa Counties. The name Miwok is derived from the word meaning "human beings" in these languages. The term has been applied to **Miwok Lake** [Yosemite N.P.] and to **Mi-Wuk Village** [Tuolumne Co.].

MOCCASIN (MAHK uh suhn) CREEK [Tuolumne Co.]. Named not for a type of shoe, but because miners mistook harmless local snakes for the poisonous water moccasin found in the southern United States. The term for the Indian footwear is derived from an Algonquian language of Virginia.

MOCHO (MOH choh), ARROYO [Alameda Co.]. The Spanish term means "cut-off creek," referring to the creek's having no outlet. It has sometimes been confused with Spanish *macho,* meaning both "masculine" and "mule."

MODESTO (muh DES toh, moh DES toh) [Stanislaus Co.]. In 1870 the town was supposed to be named for the railroad magnate William C. Ralston; when he declined the honor, the name was changed to the Spanish word for "modest."

MODJESKA (moh JES kuh) CANYON [Orange Co.]. Named for the Polish actress Helena Modjeska, who lived in the area in the 1870s.

MODOC (MOH dahk). Refers to an Indian tribe who lived in Siskiyou and Modoc Counties and the adjacent part of Oregon, and to their language; they were related to the Klamath tribe of Oregon. The Modoc became famous for holding out against the U.S. Army in the Modoc War of the 1870s. The name is derived from *moowat'aakknii,* meaning "southerners" in the Klamath language. **Modoc County** was named after the tribe in 1874.

MOJAVE (muh HAH vee). Also spelled Mohave, the term refers to an Indian tribe of the Yuman family, living on the Colorado River in San Bernardino County and the adjacent area of Arizona, and to their language. The term is derived from their name for themselves, *hamakháav.* The **Mojave Desert** and **River** [San Bernardino Co.] were named after them, and the town of **Mojave** [Kern Co.] was named after the desert in 1876. The spelling with *j* is official for the California places and for the Mojave Tribe; but the spelling with *h* is official for Mohave County in Arizona.

MOKELUMNE (moh KEL uh mee, moh KAHL uh mee) **RIVER** [Amador, Calaveras, San Joaquin Cos.]. The name is Plains Miwok, containing the suffix *-umne,* "people of"; the stem may be *moke,* "fishnet." **Mokelumne Hill** [Calaveras Co.] was named after the river around 1850.

MOLATE (moh LAH tee) **POINT** [Contra Costa Co.]. A corruption of Spanish *moleta,* "muller"—that is, a stone used for grinding pigments.

MOLINO (muh LEE noh) [Sonoma Co.]. On the Molino land grant of 1836. It may be a Spanish family name, or it may reflect Spanish *molino,* "mill."

MONACHE (moh NACH ee, MOH nuh chee). Refers to an Indian tribe and language, also called Mono, belonging to the Numic branch of the Uto-Aztecan family; the tribe lives in Madera, Mono, and Inyo Counties. The name is taken from the neighboring Yokuts language, in which the Monache were called *monachi,* "fly people," because they commonly ate the pupae of a fly found on the shores of inland lakes. The tribe gives its name to the settlement called **Monachee** [Inyo Co.]. The alternative form Mono was used to name **Mono** (MOH noh) **Lake** in 1852, and **Mono County** was created in 1861. The pronunciation *MAH noh* for the lake is now popular among airline pilots who fly over the area, perhaps by confusion with the abbreviated name for the disease mononucleosis.

MONROVIA [Los Angeles Co.]. A Latinized form derived from the name of William N. Monroe, the engineer who laid out the town in 1886.

MONTALVO (mahn TAL voh) [Ventura Co.]. Named in 1887 for Garci Rodríguez de Montalvo, the sixteenth-century Spanish writer in whose romantic fiction the name California first appeared, referring to a kingdom of beautiful black Amazons.

MONTAÑA DE ORO (mahn TAN uh dee OR oh, mohn TAHN yuh . . .) [San Luis Obispo Co.]. The name literally means "mountain of gold" but refers to the blaze of spring flowers.

MONTARA (mahn TAH ruh), **POINT** [San Mateo Co.]. The name was recorded as Montoro in 1867; it is probably a corruption of a Spanish word such as *montosa,* "forested."

MONTE. Originally a Spanish word for "mountain"; in modern times it more commonly means "bushes, forest." The word is found with both meanings in many California place names—for example, **Monte Rio** (mahn tee REE oh) [Sonoma Co.], intended to mean "river mountain"; **Monte Sano** (SAH noh) [Sonoma Co.], for "healthy mountain"; **Monte Vista** [Santa Clara Co.], suggesting "mountain view"; and **Monte Nido** (NEE doh) [Los Angeles Co.], for "mountain nest."

MONTEBELLO (mahn tuh BEL oh) [Los Angeles Co.]. Italian (rather than Spanish) for "beautiful mountain," so named in 1887.

MONTECITO (mahn tuh SEE toh) [Santa Barbara Co.]. Spanish for "little forest." The name was given in 1783 to what is now the site of Santa Barbara Mission; later it was applied to the present location.

MONTE CRISTO [Sonoma Co.]. Italian for "mount (of) Christ," taken from Alexandre Dumas's famous novel *The Count of Monte Cristo.*

MONTEREY (mahn tuh RAY) **BAY.** Named in 1602 in honor of Gaspar de Zúñiga y Acevedo, Count of Monterey, who was then viceroy of New Spain. The name stands for *monte del rey,* "mountain/forest of the king"; the city of Monterrey, Mexico, shows the modern Spanish spelling of the same name. The California town of **Monterey** was founded in 1770, and **Monterey County** was named in 1850. Monterey Jack cheese, named for its producer, David Jacks, is said to be the only native California cheese.

MONTEZUMA (mahn tuh ZOO muh) [Solano Co.; Tuolumne Co.]. The name of the Aztec king at the time when Cortés invaded Mexico; the Aztec original is *Motecuzoma,* "angry lord." In 1827 the provincial legislature resolved that Alta California should be renamed Montezuma, but the proposal was rejected by the Mexican government.

MORAGA (muh RAG uh, muh RAH guh) [Contra Costa Co.]. Named in 1886 for the landowner Joaquín Moraga, son of the explorer Gabriel Moraga.

MORENO (muh REE noh) [Riverside Co.]. A Spanish word for "brown," in this case referring to Frank E. Brown, a founder of the community.

MORGAN HILL [Santa Clara Co.]. Named around 1892, not in reference to a hill, but after a landowner whose name was Morgan Hill.

MORONGO (muh RAHNG goh) **VALLEY** [San Bernardino Co.]. Named for *maronga,* a Serrano Indian village.

Morongo Indian Reservation [Riverside Co.] was so named when people from Morongo Valley moved here in the mid nineteenth century.

MORO ROCK [Sequoia N.P.]. The Mexican Spanish word *moro* refers to the type of horse called a blue roan; the earlier meaning is "a Moor" (i.e., a North African Arab). In several California place names, *moro* has sometimes been confused with *morro,* "crown-shaped rock."

MORRO ROCK and **BAY** [San Luis Obispo Co.]. From the Spanish *morro,* "crown-shaped rock," applied here in 1769.

MOTHER LODE. Early miners believed erroneously that a huge vein of gold extended from the Middle Fork of the American River to a point near Mariposa. Although this idea has long since been discarded by geologists, the name continues to be applied to the area.

MOUNT BALDY [San Bernardino Co.]. Named after nearby Old Baldy peak, also called San Antonio Peak; but Mount Baldy refers to the community rather than the mountain.

MUAH (MOO uh) **MOUNTAIN** [Inyo Co.]. Probably from Panamint *mïa,* "moon."

MUGU (muh GOO), **POINT** [Ventura Co.]. This name was recorded by Spanish explorers of 1542 and so may have the distinction of being the oldest native Californian name in continuous written use. It was applied to a Chumash village that the Spanish called *muwu,* "beach."

MUIR (MYOO uhr) **BEACH** and **WOODS** [Marin Co.]. Named for the naturalist, mountaineer, and author John Muir (1838–1914), the father of the conservation movement in California, and the founder of the Sierra Club. His name has also been applied to many other places in the state; at one time a proposed superhighway across the Sierras was jokingly labeled the John Muir Freeway.

MUROC (MYOO rahk) [Kern Co.]. Named in 1910 by spelling backward the surname of the settlers Clifford and Ralph Corum.

MURPHYS [Calaveras Co.]. Named in 1848 for the miner John M. Murphy, who was later mayor of the city of San Jose.

MURRIETA (mer ee ET uh) [Riverside Co.]. Named about 1885 for the landowner John Murrieta. The name should not be confused with Joaquín Murieta, a name that was applied to several bandits active in northern California during the 1850s and that survives in **Joaquin Murieta Caves** [Alameda Co.]. After a man claiming to be the bandit was captured and decapitated by California rangers in 1853, there arose a romantic legend of Joaquín Murieta as a Robin Hood–like figure.

NACIMIENTO (nah suh mee EN toh) **RIVER** [San Luis Obispo, Monterey Cos.]. The Spanish word, meaning "birth," can refer both to the source of a stream and to the Nativity of Christ. In 1769, explorers who camped near here recorded that they were near the *nacimiento* of a stream. A later expedition, in 1774, apparently thought their predecessors had given the stream the name *Nacimiento,* "Nativity."

NAPA (NAP uh). The name has been recorded for the **Napa Valley** area since 1823; it may be a Patwin word for "grizzly bear." The city was founded and given this name in 1848, and **Napa County,** famous for its wine, was named in 1850.

NARANJO (nuh RAHN hoh) [Tulare Co.]. Spanish for "orange tree" (the fruit is *naranja*); the name was applied here around 1904.

NATAQUA. A territory in northeastern California that settlers declared independent in 1855; the name is of unknown origin. In 1863, the area, now known as **Honey Lake Valley** [Lassen Co.], became the topic of dispute between California and Nevada in what is known as the Sagebrush War.

NATIONAL CITY [San Diego Co.]. Represents an adaptation of Spanish Rancho de la Nación, "ranch of the nation," the land grant on which the town was founded in 1871.

NATOMA (nuh TOH muh) [Sacramento Co.]. From the name of a Nisenan Indian village called *notoma,* "east place, upstream place." The name was given to the heroine of Victor Herbert's opera *Natoma,* now seldom performed.

NAUFUS (NAY fuhs) **CREEK** [Trinity Co.]. The Wintu name, referring to a local Indian band, was *norboos,* "those living to the south."

NAVALENCIA (nay vuh LEN shuh) [Fresno Co.]. A combination of the names of two varieties of oranges: navel and Valencia.

NAVARRO (nuh VAH roh) **RIVER** [Mendocino Co.]. The original name was probably Indian, but it was assimilated to Spanish Navarra, a province in Spain, or Navarro, a family name.

NAWTAWAKET (NAW tuh wah kuht) **CREEK** [Shasta Co.]. The name reflects Wintu *noti waqat,* "south creek."

NEEDLES [San Bernardino Co.]. Named in 1883 after the nearby pinnacles on the Arizona side of the Colorado River.

NEGIT (NEG it) **ISLAND** [Mono Co.]. The name is from Eastern Mono *nïkïtta,* "goose."

NEVADA CITY [Nevada Co.]. The name was first applied in 1850, based on the name Sierra Nevada, which in Spanish means "snowy range," from *nieve,* "snow." **Nevada County** was named after the city on April 25, 1851. The city and county were *not* named after the state of Nevada, which was named independently in 1864 after the Sierra Nevada. The name of **Nevada Fall** [Yosemite N.P.] was inspired by the meaning "snowy."

NEVAHBE (nuh VAH bee) **RIDGE** [Mono Co.]. The name is from Mono *nïpapi,* "snow," pronounced approximately *nuh VAH vee.*

NEW CAMALDOLI (kuh MAHL doh lee) [Monterey Co.]. The site of the Immaculate Heart Hermitage, founded by Camaldolese monks. The name is from Camaldoli, a hermitage near Florence, Italy.

NEWHALL [Los Angeles Co.]. Named in 1876 for the landowner Henry M. Newhall.

NEW HELVETIA [Sacramento Co.]. The settlement was founded by John Sutter in 1839 and was given the Latin name for Switzerland, the land of Sutter's ancestors.

NEWPORT [Orange Co.]. Named in 1870 because it was a "new port" between Los Angeles and San Diego.

NICASIO (nuh KASH oh, nuh KAHZ ee oh) [Marin Co.]. The term was applied in an 1835 land grant; it probably referred to a local Indian who had been baptized with the name of Saint Nicasius.

NICE (NEES) [Lake Co.]. Named around 1928 after Nice on the French Riviera.

NICOLAUS (NIK uh luhs) [Sutter Co.]. With a change in spelling, named for an early settler from Germany, Nicholaus Allgeier, who ran a ferry on the Feather River.

NILAND (NIGH luhnd) [Imperial Co.]. The name was coined in 1916 from "Nile-land," referring to the fertility of the Nile Valley in Egypt.

NIMSHEW (NIM shoo) [Butte Co.]. The name is from Konkow (Maidu) *nem sewi*, "big stream."

NIPINNAWASEE (nuh pin uh WAH see) [Madera Co.]. A name imported from Michigan, where it is said to mean "many deer" in an Algonquian language.

NIPOMO (nuh POH moh) [San Luis Obispo Co.]. From Obispeño Chumash *nipumu'*, "house place, village."

NIPPLE. The name of this body part has been given to prominences in several parts of the state, such as **Nellie's Nipple** [Kern Co.].

NISENAN (NIS uh nan). Refers to an Indian tribe and language of the Maidu family; tribe members live in Sacramento, Placer, and El Dorado Counties.

NISENE (nigh SEEN) **MARKS STATE PARK** [Santa Cruz Co.]. Named in 1963 for Nisene Marks, the mother of the donors of the property.

NOB HILL [San Francisco Co.]. Perhaps from the slang word *nob*, "person of wealth and importance," because rich people lived there. The term may be from *nabob*, referring to an East Indian potentate, from Persian *nawâb*.

NOE (NOH ee) **VALLEY** [San Francisco Co.]. Named for José Noé, the last *alcalde*, or mayor, of San Francisco under Mexican rule.

NOJOGUI (noh HOH wee) **CREEK** [Santa Barbara Co.]. The name is that of a Chumash village, written by the Spanish as Najague, Najajue, Na-jao-ui, Nojogue, Nojoque, or Najoqui. The original meaning is unknown.

NOMLAKI (NOHM lah kee). Refers to an Indian tribe of the Wintu family and their language, once spoken in the Tehama County area; the name means something like "west speech." The site of a former Indian reservation preserves the place name **Nome-Lackee.**

NOMWAKET (NOHM wah kuht) **CREEK** [Shasta Co.]. From Wintu *nom-waqat,* "west creek."

NOPAH (NOH pah) **RANGE** [Inyo Co.]. Local people claim this means "no water," from English *no* plus Paiute *paa,* "water."

NORCO [Riverside Co.]. An acronym coined from *North Corona Land Company* in 1922.

NORTH BEACH [San Francisco Co.]. Once at the northern end of San Francisco, until landfill expanded the city area.

NORTH BLOOMFIELD [Nevada Co.]. Miners wanted to call the town Bloomfield in the 1850s, but there was already a Bloomfield in Sonoma County, so the name North Bloomfield was adopted. Similarly, **North San Juan** [Nevada Co.] was so named in 1857 because of San Juan (Bautista) in San Benito County.

NOSONI (nuh SOH nee) **CREEK** [Shasta Co.]. From Wintu *no-sono,* "south peak."

NOVATO (nuh VAH toh) [Marin Co.]. Named after a leader of the Miwok Indians, who had probably been given the name of Saint Novatus at his baptism.

NOYO (NOY oh) **RIVER** [Mendocino Co.]. A Northern Pomo village name, from *nó,* "dust, ashes," plus *yow,* "under, in."

NUBIEBER (NOO bee ber) [Lassen Co.]. Represents "New Bieber," named after the nearby town of Bieber.

NUEVO (noo AY voh, NWAY voh) [Riverside Co.]. From the Rancho San Jacinto Nuevo y Potrero, "Ranch of New San Jacinto and (the) Pasture," a land grant of 1846.

OAKLAND [Alameda Co.]. Called Encinal, "live-oak grove," in Spanish times. The modern name was given in 1850.

OCEANO (oh see AN oh) [San Luis Obispo Co.]. Spanish for "ocean"; the name was given around 1893.

OCOTILLO (ah kuh TIL oh, oh kuh TEE yoh) [Imperial Co.]. Named for a flowering desert shrub. The term is a diminutive of Mexican Spanish *ocote,* "pine tree, firewood," itself a borrowing from Aztec *ocotl,* "pine tree."

OHLONE (oh LOHN). Refers to Indian tribes of the Costanoan family and their languages, once spoken in San Francisco and Alameda Counties and adjacent areas; the term is from the native tribal name *olxon.*

OJAI (OH high) [Ventura Co.]. A Chumash village name, identified as *ahwai,* "moon."

OLANCHA (oh LAN chuh) [Inyo Co.]. Supposedly named for a Panamint Indian band living south of Owens Lake.

OLD BALDY [San Bernardino Co.]. A local name for San Antonio Peak. Similarly, nearby San Gorgonio Peak is often called **Old Grayback**; the word *grayback* refers to a body louse. **Old Saddleback** [Orange Co.] is a mountain shaped like a saddle; its two peaks are called Santiago and Modjeska.

OLEMA (oh LEE muh) [Marin Co.]. Named after a Coast Miwok village, probably derived from *óle,* "coyote."

OLEUM (OH lee uhm) [Contra Costa Co.]. Named around 1912 by abbreviating the word *petroleum.*

OLINDA (oh LIN duh) [Orange Co.]. Named after Olinda on the island of Maui, Hawaii; that in turn was named after a town in Brazil.

OLIVENHAIN (oh LEE vuhn hine) [San Diego Co.]. Originally a German settlement. Although the name is German for "olive grove," it may originally have been Olivenheim, "olive home."

OLOMPALI (uh LAHM puh lee, oh lum PAH lee) [Marin Co.]. Named for a Coast Miwok village called *óolum pálli,* apparently containing *ólom,* "south." The Battle of Olompali was an episode in the Bear Flag Revolt of 1846, when Anglo-Americans established a "Republic of California" for one month; subsequently the United States conquered the state as part of the Mexican War.

OMENOKU (ah muh NOH koo) [Humboldt Co.]. This small promontory north of Trinidad Head retains its Yurok name, *o-menoku,* "where it projects."

OMO (OH moh) **RANCH** [El Dorado Co.]. Named for an Indian village. It may be an abbreviation of Northern Sierra Miwok *oomu'a'koča,* the name of the hut in which Indian women were sequestered during their menstrual periods.

ONE SUERTE (wuhn soo AIR tee) [Monterey Co.]. The English word *one* plus Spanish *suerte,* "chance, luck," used in Mexican California to mean "a farming lot located near a town."

ONO (OH noh) [Shasta Co.]. Named in 1883 for a town mentioned in 1 Chronicles.

ONTARIO [San Bernardino Co.]. Named in 1882 for the Canadian province of Ontario—said to be from an Iroquoian word meaning "lake fine."

OPHIR (OH fer) [Placer Co.]. Named after a land of gold mentioned repeatedly in the Bible.

ORANGE [Orange Co.]. The city was named in 1873, in recognition of the citrus industry. **Orange County** was formed in 1889. In the Sierra foothills, **Orange Cove** [Fresno Co.] was named in 1913.

OREGON HOUSE [Yuba Co.]. Named for the state of Oregon. The state's name may derive from a misreading of Ouariconsint, a form of the name Wisconsin given on a 1715 map; the ultimate origin is in an Algonquian language.

ORESTIMBA (or uhs TEEM buh) **CREEK** [Stanislaus Co.]. The name, first recorded in 1810, apparently contains Costanoan *ores,* "bear."

ORICK [Humboldt Co.]. From the Yurok Indian village name *oo'rekw.*

ORINDA (or IN duh) [Contra Costa Co.]. So named in the 1880s. The name may have been coined for its pleasing sound, or it may have been taken from a nineteenth-century literary work.

ORLEANS [Humboldt Co.]. Settled in 1850 and called New Orleans Bar, probably after the city in Louisiana.

ORO. The Spanish word for "gold" was a favorite for naming places in nineteenth-century California, and it occurs in many names, such as **Oro Fino** (or oh FEE noh) [Siskiyou Co.], meaning "fine gold"; **Oro Grande** (GRAN dee) [San Bernardino Co.], "big gold"; and **Oro Loma** (LOH muh) [Fresno Co.], intended for "gold hill." **Oroville** (OR oh vil, OR uh vil) [Butte Co.] was so named in 1855. The name of the **Orocopia Mountains** [Riverside Co.] suggests a wealth of gold (Latin *copia,* "abundance").

OROSI (oh ROH suh) [Tulare Co.]. A name coined in 1888 on the basis of Spanish *oro,* "gold," because the fields around were covered with golden poppies.

OSO. The Spanish word for "bear" occurs in a number of place names. **Oso Flaco** (oh soh FLAH koh) **Lake** [San Luis Obispo Co.], named in 1769, refers to a "lean bear" killed by the Spanish soldiers. **Los Osos Valley** [San Luis Obispo Co.] was famous for its numerous grizzlies; **Cañada de los Osos** [Santa Clara Co.] also means "valley of the bears."

OTAY (oh TIE, OH tie) [San Diego Co.]. The name of an Indian village, perhaps from Diegueño *'etaay,* "big."

OWENS LAKE [Inyo Co.]. Named in 1845 for Richard Owens, of Ohio, a member of Frémont's expedition (1845–46).

OWENYO (OH uhn yoh) [Inyo Co.]. Coined in 1905 by combining the names Owens (Lake) and Inyo (County).

OXNARD [Ventura Co.]. Named around 1900 for Henry T. Oxnard, who had established a beet-sugar refinery here. The surname is originally from "oxen-herd," meaning a herder of oxen.

PACHECO (puh CHAY koh) [Contra Costa Co.]. Named for the landowner Salvio Pacheco in 1858. However, **Pacheco Pass** [Santa Clara Co.], a term recorded since 1848, refers to the rancho owners Francisco and Juan Pacheco.

PACIFICA (puh SIF uh kuh) [San Mateo Co.]. In 1957 the shore communities of Linda Mar, Sharp Park, Edgemar, Westview, Pacific Manor, Rockaway Beach, Fairway Park, Vallemar, and Pedro Point were incorporated as a city, named after the Pacific Ocean. The name of the ocean is frequent elsewhere, as in **Pacific Grove** [Monterey Co.], **Pacific Beach** [San Diego Co.], and **Pacific Palisades** [Los Angeles Co.].

PACOIMA (puh KOY muh) [Los Angeles Co.]. The Gabrielino name may mean "running water."

PAHRUMP (PAH rump) [Inyo Co.]. From Southern Paiute *pa-rïmpa,* "water mouth."

PAICINES (pie SEE nuhs) [San Benito Co.]. Reflects an Indian village name, perhaps from Mutsun (Costanoan) *paysen,* "to get pregnant."

PAIUTE (PIE yoot). Also spelled Piute. The term is popularly applied to several related Indian tribes whose languages belong to the Numic branch of the Uto-Aztecan family; the tribes live in eastern California and in the Great Basin. These include the Northern Paiute or Paviotso of northwestern California (plus adjacent Oregon and Nevada), the Owens Valley Paiute (or Eastern Mono) of California, and the Southern Paiute, including the Chemehuevi, of southeastern California (plus southern Nevada and southern Utah). The term *Paiute* has been said to mean "water Ute" or "true Ute"; however, the term *Ute* (for a neighboring tribe, after whom the state of Utah is named) is from Spanish *yuta,* whereas *Paiute* is from Spanish *payuchis,* probably from Southern Paiute *payuutsi,* "Paiute Indian." By false analogy, the English term *Paiute* has been made to resemble the tribal name of the Utes. The term occurs in many place names such as

Piute Creek [Lassen Co.], **Piute Mountain** [Mono Co.], and **Piute Range** [San Bernardino Co.].

PAJARO (PAH huh roh) **RIVER** [Santa Cruz, Monterey Cos.]. The name, from Spanish *pájaro,* "bird," was given by the Spanish in 1769 when they saw a stuffed bird erected by local Indians.

PALA (PAH luh) [San Diego Co.]. From Luiseño *páala,* "water."

PALISADE. A term used to refer to various types of steep elevation, such as the peaks called **North** and **Middle Palisade** [Kings Canyon N.P.], or the cliffs that give their name to **Pacific Palisades** [Los Angeles Co.].

PALM [Riverside Co.]. When this word appears in place names, it usually refers to the native California fan palm, *Washingtonia filifera,* which is abundant around desert oases such as **Palm Springs** and **Thousand Palms** [Riverside Co.] or **Twentynine Palms** [San Bernardino Co.]. However, **Palmdale** [Los Angeles Co.] is named not for a true palm, but for the Joshua tree (*Yucca brevifolia*).

PALO. Spanish for "stick," but the word was used in Spanish California to mean "tree" and occurs in many place names. **Palo Alto** (pal oh AL toh) [Santa Clara Co.] means "tall tree" referring to a large redwood. **Palo Verde** (VER dee) [Imperial Co.], literally, "green tree," is the name of a desert tree with green bark; however, **Palos Verdes** [Los Angeles Co.] refers not to the desert tree, but to "green trees" in general. **Palo Escrito** (es KREE toh) **Peak** [Monterey Co.] refers to a "written tree"—that is, one with carvings on its bark.

PALOMAR. Spanish for "pigeon roost, dovecote," from *paloma,* "dove, pigeon." Both Spanish words have often been used in place names. **Paloma** (puh LOH muh) is a settlement in Calaveras County. **Palomar** (PAL uh mahr) **Mountain** [San Diego Co.] takes its name from **Palomar Creek** and the Palomar land grant, recorded in 1846.

PAMO (PAH moh) **VALLEY** [San Diego Co.]. From a Diegueño village name, *paamuu,* of unknown meaning.

PANAMINT (PAN uh mint). Refers to a tribe of Inyo County and their language, which belongs to the Numic branch of the Uto-Aztecan family; the tribe and language are also called Koso, Tïmpisa, and California Shoshoni. The probable origin of the term is Southern Paiute *panïwïntsi,* "water person." The name has also been given to **Panamint Valley** [Inyo Co.].

PANOCHE (puh NOH chee, puh NOHCH) [San Benito Co.]. From Mexican Spanish *panoche* or *panocha,* referring to a kind of raw sugar, sometimes made from wild plant foods.

PAOHA (pah OH huh, pay OH huh) **ISLAND** [Mono Co.]. From Eastern Mono *pa-ohaa,* "water baby," referring to a dangerous supernatural creature supposed to live in bodies of water.

PARAISO (puh RIE zoh, pah ruh EE soh) **SPRINGS** [Monterey Co.]. From Spanish *paraíso,* "paradise."

PARKER DAM [San Bernardino Co.]. Named for Parker, a railroad station in Arizona, which in turn was named after Earl H. Parker, a Santa Fe Railroad employee.

PASADENA (pas uh DEE nuh) [Los Angeles Co.]. In 1875, early settlers sought an Indian name for the new community, hoping to express the notion of "valley." One of them wrote to a friend who was a missionary among the Chippewa Indians in the upper Mississippi Valley, and was given the term *weoquân pâ sâ de ná,* "crown of the valley"—which was shortened to Pasadena. The

Chippewa prototype is said to be *passadina,* "there is a valley."

PASKENTA (pas KEN tuh) [Tehama Co.]. From Wintu *phas kenti,* "under the cliff."

PASO. Spanish for "pass, passage, crossing, ford, channel"; the word appears in many place names. **Paso Robles** (pas uh ROH buhlz) [San Luis Obispo Co.] is short for Paso de Robles, "passage of (the) oaks," referring to the deciduous oak called *roble* in Spanish (the live oak is *encina,* represented in other place names).

PATCHEN PASS [Santa Clara, Santa Cruz Cos.]. Named for a famous racehorse with the improbable name of George M. Patchen.

PATTYMOCUS (PAT ee mah kuhs) [Tehama Co.]. Said to be a Wintu name referring to the shape of a tipped-over basket.

PATWIN (PAT win). Refers to a tribe of Colusa and Yolo Counties and their language, which belongs to the Wintun family. The term means "human being" in the Patwin language.

PAUMA (PAW muh) [San Diego Co.]. From a Luiseño Indian village name, probably *páamay,* "little water."

PAUTAH COUNTY. A California county from 1852 to 1859, when it became part of what is now the state of Nevada. It was adjacent to what is now northeastern California.

PEANUT [Trinity Co.]. Named around 1898 by the Weaverville postmaster. He was asked to suggest a name and was eating peanuts at the time.

PECONOM CREEK (puh KOH nuhm) [Lassen Co.]. Named for a Maidu Indian woman, Roxie Peconom; the name is probably from Maidu *pekúnim,* "mountain lion."

PEDERNALES (ped er NAH luhs), **POINT** [Santa Barbara Co.]. The Spanish name, from *pedernal,* "flint," was given in 1769.

PENITENCIA (pen uh TEN see uh) **CREEK** [Santa Clara Co.]. The Spanish term means "penitence," and apparently referred to an adobe house once used as a confessional.

PENRYN (PEN rin) [Placer Co.]. Named after the city of Penrhyn in Wales.

PEPPERWOOD [Humboldt Co.]. Established around 1900, the town was given the local name of the California laurel or bay tree.

PERMANENTE (per muh NEN tee) **CREEK** [Santa Clara Co.]. The Spanish word for "permanent" refers to a creek that, unlike many California streams, does not dry up in the summer.

PERRIS (PAIR uhs) [Riverside Co.]. Named in 1886 for Fred T. Perris, one of the founders.

PESCADERO (pes kuh DAIR oh) [San Mateo Co.]. Spanish for "fishing place," from *pescar,* "to fish."

PETALUMA (pet uh LOO muh) [Sonoma Co.]. From Coast Miwok *péta lúuma,* "hillside back" (i.e., hillside ridge).

PETROLIA [Humboldt Co.]. Originally spelled Petrolea, the name was given in 1865 when the first oil deposits to be exploited commercially in California were found near here.

PHILO (FIE loh) [Mendocino Co.]. Named after 1868 by the landowner Cornelius Prather for his favorite girl cousin, whose given name was probably Philomena.

PICACHO (puh KAH choh) **PEAK** [Imperial Co.]. A redundancy, since Spanish *picacho* itself means "peak."

PICO (PEE koh) [Los Angeles Co.]. Named in 1904 after the family of Pío Pico, the last governor of Mexican California. In 1958 the towns of Pico and Rivera incorporated under the new name **Pico Rivera**. A cousin of Pío Pico, Salomón Pico, became a highway robber; **Mount Solomon** [Santa Barbara Co.], with an English spelling, is named for him. Spanish *pico* also means "mountain peak," as in **Pico Blanco** [Monterey Co.], literally, "white peak."

PIEDMONT (PEED mahnt) [Alameda Co.]. French for "foot (of the) mountain"; the name was given around 1876 because of the foothill location.

PIEDRA (pee AY druh) [Fresno Co.]. Spanish for "stone." The term occurs in many place names, such as **Piedras Blancas** (BLANG kuhs) [San Luis Obispo Co.], literally, "white rocks"; **Piedra Gorda** (GOR duh) [Los Angeles Co.], "fat rock"; and **Piedra de Lumbre** (LOOM bree) **Canyon** [San Diego Co.], meaning "stone of fire" (i.e., flintstone).

PIGEON POINT [San Mateo Co.]. So named because the clipper ship *Carrier Pigeon* was wrecked here in 1853.

PILARCITOS (pil er SEE tohs) [San Mateo Co.]. Spanish for "little pillars" (from *pilar,* "pillar"); the name, known since 1836, refers to local pillar-shaped rock formations.

PINACATE (pee nuh KAH tee, pin uh KAH tee) [Riverside Co.]. Mexican Spanish for a type of black beetle locally called "stink bug," from Aztec *pinacatl.*

PINCHOT (PIN shoh), **MOUNT** [Kings Canyon N.P.]. Named for Gifford Pinchot, at one time chief of the U.S. Division of Forestry, later governor of Pennsylvania.

PINNACLES NATIONAL MONUMENT [San Benito Co.]. Named for its pillarlike geological formations, created by erosion.

PINO. Spanish for "pine." The word occurs in many California place names, especially in the plural form *pinos*, as in **Mount Pinos** (PIE nuhs, PEE nohs) [Ventura Co.], also called Pine Mountain. **Point Pinos** [Monterey Co.] was so named in 1602. The older pronunciation *PEE nuhs* is now usually avoided because of homophony with *penis*.

PINOLE (puh NOHL) [Contra Costa Co.]. A Mexican Spanish word for ground and toasted grain or seeds, derived from Aztec *pinolli*.

PIÑON (pin YOHN) [Riverside Co.]. Also spelled *pinyon*, the word refers to several species of pine that have edible seeds; it is from Spanish *piñón*, derived from *piña*, "pine cone." But **Pinyon Peak** [Monterey Co.] is probably from Spanish *peñón*, "large crag," since there are no piñon pines here.

PIRU (puh ROO, PEE roo, pie ROO) [Ventura Co.]. From Kitanemuk *pi'idhu-ku*, the name of a plant.

PISMO (PIZ moh) **BEACH** [San Luis Obispo Co.]. The name is from Obispeño Chumash *pismu'*, "tar, asphalt," referring to the natural oil seepage on the shoreline.

PITAS (PEE tuhs) **POINT** [Ventura Co.]. The name is a garbled form of Spanish Los Pitos, "the whistles," so named in 1769 because the Spanish were kept awake by Indians playing on whistles.

PIT RIVER [Modoc, Lassen, Shasta Cos.]. The stream was so named by Hudson's Bay Company trappers in the 1820s because the Indians dug pits on its banks to trap animals. Deer or elk antlers were embedded in the bottom of the pits, to pierce any luckless animal that might fall in. In later years the name was often spelled Pitt River and mistakenly associated with the English prime minister William Pitt.

PITTSBURG [Contra Costa Co.]. Named around 1858 for Pittsburgh, Pennsylvania, at a time when coal mining was beginning in the Mount Diablo area.

PIUTE. *See* Paiute.

PLACENTIA (pluh SEN shuh) [Orange Co.]. The school district was named in 1884 by a derivation from the Latin verb *placet*, "it is pleasant"; there was also a city named Placentia in ancient Italy, now called Piacenza.

PLACER (PLAS er). This western American term, borrowed from Spanish, refers to alluvial or glacial deposits containing gold particles; washing the gold out is called "placer mining." For a few years after 1842 a placer in Los Angeles County was worked with moderate success, and **Placerita** (plas uh REE tuh) **Creek** [Los Angeles Co.], probably from the Spanish diminutive *placerito*, recalls that early discovery of gold. **Placerville** [El Dorado Co.] was so named in 1850 because the streets were almost impassable on account of the numerous placering holes. **Placer County** was created in 1851 from parts of Sutter and Yuba Counties.

PLATINA (PLAT uh nuh) [Shasta Co.]. So named in 1921 because it is in an area rich in platinum ore. Spanish *platina*, pronounced *plah TEE nah*, is derived from *plata*, "silver," and was the name first given to platinum when it was discovered in South America.

PLAYA DEL REY [Los Angeles Co.]. Spanish for "beach of the king"; founded as a recreation area, the site was given its name in 1902.

PLEASANTON [Alameda Co.]. Named in 1867 for General Alfred Pleasonton, who fought in the Mexican War. The name was misspelled when the post office was established.

PLUMAS (PLOO muhs) COUNTY. Reflects Río de las Plumas, the Spanish name for the Feather River.

POGONIP (POH guh nip) CREEK [Santa Cruz Co.]. The term *pogonip* is used in the Great Basin for an icy fog that forms in mountain valleys; it is derived from *pakïnappï,* "cloud, fog," in Southern Paiute and other Numic languages. It is not known how the term arrived in the Santa Cruz area.

POKYWAKET (POH kee wak uht) CREEK [Shasta Co.]. From Wintu *puki waqat,* "unripe creek"; unripe acorns were brought here to be processed.

POMO (POH moh). A cover term for several related Indian tribes and languages of Mendocino, Lake, and Sonoma Counties. The name is derived from Northern Pomo *phó'ma',* "inhabitant." However, the settlement called **Pomo,** although in Pomo Indian territory, takes its name from Northern Pomo *phóomóo,* "at red-earth hole," referring to a source of magnesite.

POMONA (puh MOH nuh) [Los Angeles Co.]. The name of the Roman goddess of orchards and gardens, applied here in 1875. **Pomona College** is located in the adjacent town of Claremont.

POMPONIO (pahm POH nee oh) CREEK [San Mateo Co.]. Named for José Pomponio Lupugeyum, a Bolinas Miwok Indian, captain of a group who rebelled against the Mexican government; he was captured and executed in 1824.

POONKINY (POON kin ee) CREEK [Mendocino Co.]. From Yuki *p'unkini,* the aromatic plant called wormwood.

PORTERVILLE [Tulare Co.]. Named in 1859 by its founder, Royal Porter Putnam.

PORTOLA (por TOH luh) **VALLEY** [San Mateo Co.]. Named for Gaspar de Portolá y de Rovira, leader of the Spanish exploring expedition that entered the area in 1769.

PORTUGUESE BEND [Los Angeles Co.]. Named for Joseph Clark (Machado), a native of the Azores, who operated a fleet of whaling ships in California waters around 1860.

POSEY [Tulare Co.]. The origin is the same as that of **Poso Creek** [Kern, Tulare Cos.], from Spanish *poza, pozo,* "water hole."

POTEM (PAH tuhm) **CREEK** [Shasta Co.]. Probably takes its name from Wintu *patem,* "mountain lion."

POTRERO (poh TRAIR oh) [San Francisco Co.]. The term is Spanish for "pasture," derived from *potro,* "colt." It occurs elsewhere in many combinations such as **Potrero Chico** (CHEE koh) [Los Angeles Co.], meaning "small pasture"; and **Potrero Seco** (SAY koh) [Ventura Co.], "dry pasture."

POWAY (POW way, POW wie) [San Diego Co.]. From a Diegueño place name, *pawiiy,* which may be related to *pawiiy,* "arrowhead."

POZA; POZO. Spanish terms referring to water holes and wells; they are found in many place names, often spelled *posa, poso.* **Las Posas** (lahs POH suhs) [Ventura Co.], meaning "the water holes," is a name recorded since 1819. **Poso Creek** [Kern, Tulare Cos.] was so named in the 1850s; the settlement of **Posey** [Tulare Co.] has a variant of the same name.

PRECITA (pruh SEE tuh) **PARK** [San Francisco Co.]. From Spanish *presita,* diminutive of *presa,* "dam."

PRESIDIO (pruh SID ee oh, pruh SEE dee oh). The Spanish word means "garrison, fortified barracks"; in Spanish California it was applied to the installations at Monterey, San Diego, San Francisco, and Santa Barbara. However, **Presidio Bar** [Siskiyou Co.], also spelled Persido Bar, is an Anglicization of *pasirú'uuvree,* the name of a former Karuk Indian village nearby.

PROBERTA (proh BER tuh) [Tehama Co.]. Named in 1889 after Edward Probert.

PUENTE (poo EN tee, PWEN tee) [Los Angeles Co.]. Spanish for "bridge," the word was applied by the Portolá expedition when they had to build a bridge here in 1769. The place has also been called **La Puente,** archaic Spanish for "the bridge" (where the modern language would have *el puente*).

PUERTA DEL SUELO (PWAIR tuh del SWAY loh) [Kern Co.]. This name of a mountain pass is not Spanish for "door of the soil," as the spelling suggests, but is a garbling of *puertezuelo,* "little pass," a diminutive of *puerto,* "port, pass." Another pass, **Puerto Suelo** (PWAIR toh SWAY loh) in Monterey County, is a similar case.

PUJOL (poo HOHL) [Riverside Co.]. Named for Domingo Pujol, of Spain; it is now also pronounced *poo ZHOHL,* as if it were French.

PULGAS (PUL guhs) **CREEK** [San Mateo Co.]. Spanish *pulga,* "flea," appears in a number of California place names, applied by early travelers when they were assaulted by the insect.

PUNTA GORDA (PUN tuh GOR duh) [Humboldt Co.]. Spanish *punta* is a "point of land," and the name means "fat (or massive) point," given by a Spanish navigator to a promontory in this area in 1775.

PURISIMA (puh RIS uh muh) **MISSION** [Santa Barbara Co.]. Named for La Purísima Concepción, "the Immaculate Conception" (i.e., the conception of Mary, not of Jesus); the mission was founded in 1787. The name has also been applied to **Purisima Point** and **Hills.**

PUTAH (POO tuh) **CREEK** [Lake, Napa, Solano Cos.]. From Lake Miwok *puṭa wuwwe,* "grassy creek"; the similarity to Spanish *puta,* "whore," is purely accidental.

PYWIACK (PIE wee ak) **CASCADE** [Yosemite N.P.]. From Southern Sierra Miwok *paywayak,* the name for Vernal Falls, derived from *paywa,* "chaparral."

QUANAI (kwuh NIE) **CANYON** [San Diego Co.]. From Diegueño *kwa'naay,* "wire grass," a plant used in basket making.

QUATAL (kwuh TAHL) **CANYON** [Ventura, Santa Barbara Cos.]. This is a garbling of California Spanish *guatal,* a place where *guata,* "juniper," grows; the term is derived from Luiseño or Gabrielino *wáa'at.*

QUECHAN (kwuh CHAHN); also called Yuma. The name of an Indian tribe and language of the Yuman family, living in Imperial County and the adjacent area of Arizona. The term is derived from the native name *kwatsáan,* literally, "those who descended."

QUINADO (kee NAH doh) **CANYON** [Monterey Co.]. Probably a Spanish adaptation from the name of a Mutsun (Costanoan) Indian village, *kináw.*

QUINCY [Plumas Co.]. Named in 1854 after Quincy, Illinois, the hometown of the local hotel owner.

QUIOTA (kee OH tuh) **CREEK** [Santa Barbara Co.]. From Mexican Spanish *quiote,* a kind of yucca, from Aztec *quiotl,* "sprout."

RAMONA [San Diego Co.]. Named soon after 1884, when Helen Hunt Jackson's sentimental novel *Ramona* was at the height of its popularity. The novel's heroine was a young woman of Cahuilla Indian descent, and an outdoor Ramona Pageant is still staged annually at Hemet. The Spanish name Ramona is the feminine equivalent of Ramón, "Raymond."

RANCHO CORDOVA (kor DO vuh) [Sacramento Co.]. Not a ranch of Spanish times; the name was changed in 1955 from an earlier Cordova Village, called after the Cordova Vineyards (originally named for the Spanish city Córdoba). Similarly, **Rancho Santa Fe** [San Diego Co.] was a name given in 1906 by the Santa Fe Railroad. The railroad is named for Santa Fe, New Mexico, abbreviated from La Villa Real de la Santa Fe de San Francisco de Asís, "the royal town of the holy faith of Saint Francis of Assisi."

RANDSBURG [Kern Co.]. Named in 1895 after "The Rand," referring to the gold-mining district at Witwatersrand in the Transvaal, South Africa.

READING (RED ing) **PEAK** [Lassen N.P.]. Named in 1943 in memory of Major Pierson B. Reading, a pioneer of 1843, whose name is also associated with the town of Redding.

RED BLUFF [Tehama Co.]. Named in 1850 after the nearby reddish-colored bluffs.

REDDING [Shasta Co.]. Named in 1872 for B. B. Redding of the Central Pacific Railway. In 1874 the legislature declared that the town should be named Reading, in honor of the pioneer Major Pierson B. Reading, but the railroad refused to recognize the change. In 1880 the legislature changed the name back to Redding. However, **Redding Rock** [Humboldt Co.] was probably named for Pierson Reading, in spite of the spelling.

REDLANDS [San Bernardino Co.]. So named in 1887 for the color of the local soil.

REDONDO (ruh DAHN doh) **BEACH** [Los Angeles Co.]. Appears to mean "round beach," but it was named in 1881 for the adjacent Rancho Sausal Redondo, "round willow grove."

REDWOOD. A name applied to two species of trees: the coast redwood, *Sequoia sempervirens,* and the "big trees" of the Sierra, *Sequoiadendron giganteum.* The term appears in many place names. **Redwood City** [San Mateo Co.] was earlier known as Red Woods City (1854) because of the nearby coast redwood forest and lumbering area.

REEDLEY [Fresno Co.]. Named in 1888 for Thomas L. Reed. Since Reed objected to the use of his name, the developers added the suffix.

REFUGIO (ruh FYOO hee oh) **CREEK** [Contra Costa Co.]. The Spanish word for "refuge" refers to Nuestra Señora del Refugio, "Our Lady of Refuge."

RELIEZ (ruh LEES) **CREEK** [Monterey Co.]. From Mexican Spanish *reliz,* "landslide"; it has sometimes been interpreted as "Release Creek."

REQUA (REK wah) [Del Norte Co.]. From Yurok *rek'woy,* "river mouth."

RESEDA (ruh SEE duh) [Los Angeles Co.]. The botanical genus name for the garden plant mignonette, applied here around 1895.

REVOLON (REV uh lahn) **SLOUGH** [Ventura Co.]. Named for Jean-Marie Revolon, a French farmer in the area around 1875.

REYES (RAYZ, RAY uhz, RAY uhs), **POINT** [Marin Co.]. Named by Spanish explorers on January 6, 1603, the day of *los reyes magos,* the three Magi, who came to Bethlehem when Jesus was born. **Point Reyes National Seashore** was created in 1962.

RHEEM (REEM) [Contra Costa Co.]. Named in 1944 by the developer Donald L. Rheem.

RIALTO [San Bernardino Co.]. Named in 1887 after the business center of Venice, Italy. The Italian term corresponds to Latin *rivus altus,* "deep canal."

RICHMOND, POINT [Contra Costa Co.]. Named in 1852, the name being transferred from one of the many Richmonds in the eastern United States. The city of **Richmond,** incorporated in 1905, was named after the point.

RINCON (RING kahn) [San Diego Co.]. Spanish for "corner"; the term was commonly applied in Spanish times to pieces of land projecting into the sea or into adjacent areas. An example is **Rincon Beach** [Ventura Co.].

RIO. Spanish *río,* "river," occurs in numerous place names. **Rio Dell** (ree oh DELL) [Humboldt Co.] was called River Dell around 1890 and later was Hispanicized. **Rio Bravo** (BRAH voh) [Kern Co.] means "wild river"; it was the original name of the Kern River. **Rio Hondo** (HAHN doh) [Los Angeles Co.] means "deep river." **Rionido** (ree oh NEE doh) [Sonoma Co.], named around 1910, contains Spanish *nido,* "nest." **Rio Vista** [Solano

Co.] was named in 1860; the name is intended to mean "river view," but better Spanish would be *vista del río*. **El Rio** [Ventura Co.] means "the river," referring to the nearby Santa Clara River.

RIPON (RIP ahn) [San Joaquin Co.]. Named in 1876 for the postmaster's former home in Wisconsin; it is originally the name of a town in England.

RIVERA (ruh VAIR uh) [Los Angeles Co.]. Named in 1886, based on English *river;* however, the term is also a common Spanish family name.

RIVERSIDE. The city was named in 1871 because of the nearby Santa Ana River; **Riverside County** was named in 1893 after the city.

RIZ (RIZ) [Glenn Co.]. French for "rice," a leading crop of the area. A town in Yolo County is called **Arroz,** the Spanish equivalent.

ROBLAR (roh BLAHR) [Sonoma Co.]. Spanish for a place where *robles,* deciduous oaks, grow. The word *roble* contrasts in Spanish with *encina,* referring to the live oak.

ROCKAWAY BEACH [San Mateo Co.]. Named around 1910 for Rockaway, Long Island, a name derived from the Delaware (Algonquian) *regawihaki,* "sandy land." Folk etymology derives the name from a quarry where they take "rock away."

RODEO (roh DAY oh) [Contra Costa Co.]. A Mexican Spanish word for a roundup of cattle. When used to mean a cowboy contest, it is often pronounced (ROH dee oh). However, **Rodeo** (roh DAY oh) **Beach** [Marin Co.] is from Rodier, the name of a local family.

ROHNERVILLE [Humboldt Co.]. Named for Henry Rohner, a native of Switzerland who opened a store here in 1859.

ROMOLAND [Riverside Co.]. Founded as Romola Farms in 1925, perhaps inspired by George Eliot's novel *Romola*. Later, to avoid confusion with Ramona, the present name was substituted.

ROSEMEAD [Los Angeles Co.]. The name was applied in the 1870s to a horse farm on Leonard J. Rose's Sunny Slope estate.

ROSEVILLE [Placer Co.]. Named in 1864; the term was supposedly chosen by the residents at a picnic, in honor of the most popular girl present.

ROUGH AND READY CREEK [Tuolumne Co.]. Named for the Rough and Ready Mining Company, which had adapted the nickname of General (later President) Zachary Taylor.

RUBICON RIVER [El Dorado Co.]. Named for the ancient boundary between Italy and Gaul, crossed by Julius Caesar in 49 B.C.

RUBIDOUX (ROO buh doh), **MOUNT** [Riverside Co.]. Named for Louis Robidoux (as he spelled his name), a French pioneer.

RUMSEN (RUM suhn). Refers to the Indian tribe and language, of the Costanoan family, native to the area around Monterey Bay.

RUSSIAN RIVER [Sonoma Co.]. The Russians who settled at Fort Ross in 1812 called the river Slavyanka, "Slavic woman"; the Spanish called it Río Ruso, and the English name, a translation of the Spanish, has been in use at least since 1852.

RUWAU (ROO waw) **LAKE** [Inyo Co.]. A combination of the names of two power-company engineers, Clarence H. Rhudy and E. J. Waugh.

SACATARA (sah kuh TAIR uh) **CREEK** [Kern Co.]. Probably from the Mexican Spanish adjective *zacatero, zacatera,* "having to do with *zacate,* hay"; or from a noun, *zacatero,* "man who makes hay; a species of bird," or *zacatera,* "hayfield." Mistaken associations have been made with *secretario,* "secretary," and *sectario,* "sectarian."

SACRAMENTO (sak ruh MEN toh). The Spanish name for the Holy Sacrament was given to the Feather River in 1808 but was extended to the **Sacramento River** by 1817. The town of **Sacramento** was named in 1848, and **Sacramento County** in 1850.

SAINT GEORGE, POINT [Del Norte Co.]. Named by the British explorer George Vancouver on April 23, 1792, the day of Saint George, patron of England.

SAINT HELENA (huh LEE nuh), **MOUNT** [Sonoma, Napa and Lake Cos.]. The name was first recorded in 1851. There is a romantic story that a Russian princess named Helena planted the czar's flag on the peak in 1841. However, it is more likely that the name was given in honor of a Russian ship, the *Saint Helena,* which visited the California coast in 1841.

SAL (SAL), **POINT** [Santa Barbara Co.]. Named in 1792 for Hermenegildo Sal, the Spanish commander at San Francisco.

SALAL (suh LAL) **GULCH** [Siskiyou Co.]. Named for a shrub with edible berries. The term is derived from the Chinook Jargon language of the Pacific Northwest.

SALIDA (suh LIE duh) [Stanislaus Co.]. Spanish for "departure"; the town was named by the Southern Pacific Railroad in 1870.

SALINAN (suh LEE nuhn). Refers to a family of Indian languages once spoken in the **Salinas Valley** [Monterey Co.], but now extinct. The languages were Migueleño and Antoniano, named after the missions of San Miguel and San Antonio, respectively.

SALINAS (suh LEE nuhs) **RIVER** [Monterey Co.]. The stream was named in Spanish times for the *salinas,* "salt marshes," near its mouth. The city of **Salinas** was named in 1860.

SALSIPUEDES (sal see poo AY duhs, sal see PWAY duhs) **CREEK** [Santa Barbara Co.]. The term represents Spanish *sal si puedes,* "get out if you can," applied in many places where exit was difficult.

SALTON SEA [Riverside Co.]. The name was coined from the word *salt* and was applied to the lake bed in 1892.

SAMAGATUMA (sah muh guh TOO muh) **VALLEY** [San Diego Co.]. The name is that of a Diegueño rancheria and was written in 1845 as Jamatayune. The origin may be *'ehaa 'emat aayum,* "water place spread in the sun."

SAN ANDREAS (an DRAY uhs) [Calaveras Co.]. From Spanish San Andrés, referring to Saint Andrew the Apostle; he was supposedly crucified on an X-shaped cross, which is still called Saint Andrew's Cross. The California town was settled by Mexican miners around 1848. **San Andreas Valley** [San Mateo Co.] was named in 1774. The **San Andreas Fault,** the state's longest and best-known earthquake zone, was named after the valley in 1893.

SAN ANSELMO (an SEL moh) [Marin Co.]. The valley was called Cañada de Anselmo in 1840, apparently after an Indian who had been baptized with the name of Saint Anselm. The *San* was added to the place name later.

SAN ANTONIO RIVER [Monterey Co.]. The name refers to Saint Anthony of Padua; it was named by Father Serra in 1771, and **San Antonio Mission** was founded soon after. **San Antonio Creek** [San Bernardino Co.] was named in 1774, and the name was applied to **San Antonio Peak** in 1874. The latter is now more often called Old Baldy because of its bare top.

SAN ARDO [Monterey Co.]. Named in 1886 after the San Bernardo (Saint Bernard) Ranch; the term was later shortened to Ardo, to avoid confusion with San Bernardino.

SAN BENITO. Refers to Saint Benedict, founder of the Benedictine Order. **San Benito Valley** was named in 1772; **San Benito County** was created in 1874.

SAN BERNARDINO (ber nuh DEE noh). Named in 1819 after Saint Bernardino of Siena. **San Bernardino County** was created in 1853. The nickname "San Berdoo" is occasionally used.

SAN BERNARDO (ber NAHR doh) VALLEY [San Diego Co.]. Takes its name from Rancho San Bernardo, which was named in turn for Saint Bernard of Clairvaux.

SAN BRUNO [San Mateo Co.]. Refers to Saint Bruno of Cologne, founder of the Carthusian Order. The name was applied to **San Bruno Creek** in 1774, to **San Bruno Mountain** by the 1820s, and to the town of **San Bruno** by the 1860s.

SAN BUENAVENTURA (bway nuh ven TOO ruh) [Ventura Co.]. Named for Saint Bonaventure, an Italian of the thirteenth century; the mission was established in 1782. The name was later shortened in common usage to Ventura.

SAN CARLOS (KAHR lohs) [San Mateo Co.]. Named in 1887 to recall a supposed historical incident: It was believed that Spanish explorers first saw San Francisco Bay on November 4, 1769, the feast day of Saint Charles

Borromeo, from the hills behind the present town. Saint Charles was archbishop of Milan in the sixteenth century. **San Carlos Borromeo** (bor uh MAY oh) **Mission** [Monterey Co.] was established in 1770; it is now generally known as Mission Carmel.

SAN CARPOFORO (kahr POH fuh roh) CREEK [Monterey, San Luis Obispo Cos.]. Named in the 1830s for Saint Carpophorus. The name has been corrupted as San Carpoco, San Carpojo, Zanjapoco, and Zanjapojo, the last two by contamination with Spanish *zanja,* "ditch."

SAN CAYETANO (kah yuh TAH noh) MOUNTAIN [Ventura Co.]. Takes its name from Saint Cajetan (or Gaetano), an Italian of the sixteenth century.

SAN CLEMENTE (kluh MEN tee) ISLAND [Channel Islands, Los Angeles Co.]. Named in 1602 after Saint Clement, who was pope during the first century. The town of **San Clemente** [Orange Co.] was named in 1925 after the island.

SAN DIEGO (dee AY goh). The name refers not, as is sometimes thought, to Saint James (*Santiago* in Spanish), but rather to Saint Didacus, a Spanish holy man of the fifteenth century. The name was given in 1602 to **San Diego Bay,** and in 1769 to **San Diego Mission.** The nucleus of the present city of **San Diego** was laid out in 1850, and **San Diego County** was created in the same year. **San Dieguito** (dee uh GEE toh) [San Diego Co.], the diminutive form of this name, recorded in 1778, does not refer to a saint named Dieguito, but rather to "little San Diego."

SAN DIMAS (DEE muhs) [Los Angeles Co.]. Named for Saint Dismas, the penitent thief who was crucified at the side of Christ.

SANEL (suh NEL) [Mendocino Co.]. The earlier name of the town now called Hopland; it is from the Central Pomo village name *šanel,* meaning "at the ceremonial house." The name of **Sanel Mountain** is from the same source.

SAN ELIJO (uh LEE hoh) [San Diego Co.]. The place was named San Alejo in 1769, referring to Saint Alexius, who lived in the seventh century. The name was later confused with San Eligio, Saint Eligius or Eloi, the patron of goldsmiths.

SAN EMIGDIO (uh MEE dee oh) [Kern Co.]. Also spelled Emidio, it was named for Saint Emygdius (or Emidius), a German martyr; he is supposed to provide protection from earthquakes, which are frequent in this region.

SAN FELIPE (fuh LEE pay) [San Diego Co.]. Named in 1782 for Saint Philip, to whom Jesus spoke the words, "I am the way . . . " He was later crucified in Asia Minor. **San Felipe** [Santa Clara Co.] also honors this or another saint named Philip.

SAN FERNANDO (fer NAN doh) [Los Angeles Co.]. Named for Saint Ferdinand of Spain, who ruled as Ferdinand III of Castile and León in the thirteenth century. The mission was named for him in 1797.

SAN FRANCISCO. Refers to Saint Francis of Assisi—an especially important saint for California because the Franciscan Order, which he founded in the thirteenth century, was entrusted by the Spanish government with the spiritual care of California. **San Francisco Bay** was so named in 1595. The mission was dedicated in 1776 as La Misión de Nuestro Seráfico Padre San Francisco de Asís a la Laguna de los Dolores, "the mission of our seraphic father Saint Francis of Assisi at the Lake of [Our Lady of] the Sorrows"; for this reason it is still called Dolores

Mission. A village at Yerba Buena Cove, founded in 1835, eventually became the main settlement of the area and was given the name San Francisco in 1847. **San Francisco County,** which is coterminous with the city, was named in 1850. **San Francisco Solano** refers to Saint Francis Solanus, a Spaniard of the sixteenth century; this name was applied to the mission founded in 1823 in what is now Sonoma County, now usually called Sonoma Mission.

SAN FRANCISQUITO (fran suh SKEE toh) [San Mateo, Santa Clara Cos.]. A Spanish diminutive form meaning not Saint Little-Francis, but Little San Francisco—little, that is, in comparison with the settlement at Dolores Mission. The same name occurs in Monterey and Los Angeles Counties.

SAN GABRIEL (GAY bree uhl) [Los Angeles Co.]. Refers to the Archangel Gabriel; the name was given to the **San Gabriel Valley** in 1769, to **San Gabriel Mission** in 1771, to the **San Gabriel River** around 1782, to the **San Gabriel Mountains** around 1806, and to the town of **San Gabriel** in 1854.

SAN GERONIMO (juh RAHN uh moh) [Marin Co.]. Spanish for Saint Jerome; the name dates from 1844.

SAN GORGONIO (gor GOH nee oh) **PASS** [Riverside Co.]. Refers to Saint Gorgonius, a martyr of the third century; the name dates from 1824. The present-day **San Gorgonio Mountain** has also been called Grayback.

SAN GREGORIO (gruh GOR ee oh) [San Mateo Co.]. Named around 1830 for a pope, Saint Gregory the Great, of the sixth and seventh centuries.

SANHEDRIN (SAN hee drin) **MOUNTAIN** [Mendocino Co.]. The name was transferred by settlers from Missouri; the term originally refers to the supreme council of the ancient Hebrews.

SAN JACINTO (juh SIN toh, huh SIN toh) [Riverside Co.]. Named for Saint Hyacinth of Silesia, who lived in the thirteenth century.

SAN JOAQUIN (wah KEEN). Refers to Saint Joachim, the father of the Virgin Mary. The **San Joaquin River** was named around 1809, and **San Joaquin County** in 1850. The term **San Joaquin Valley** came into use around 1854.

SAN JOSE (hoh ZAY, oh ZAY) [Santa Clara Co.]. Refers to Saint Joseph, the husband of the Virgin Mary; the town was founded in 1777. The associated mission, known as **Mission San Jose,** is in Alameda County.

SAN JUAN BAUTISTA (wahn baw TEES tuh) [San Benito Co.]. Refers to Saint John the Baptist; the mission was founded in 1797, and the modern town in 1852.

SAN JUAN CAPISTRANO (kap uh STRAN oh, kap uh STRAH noh) [Orange Co.]. Refers to the fighting priest Saint John Capistran, who took a heroic part in defending Vienna against the Turks in the fifteenth century. The mission was founded in 1776, the modern town in 1867.

SAN LEANDRO (lee AN droh) [Alameda Co.]. Refers to Saint Leander, archbishop of Seville in the sixth century. **San Leandro Creek** was named in 1828; the town was laid out in the 1850s.

SAN LORENZO (luh REN zoh) [Alameda Co.]. Named sometime before 1812 in honor of Saint Laurence, martyred in the third century. The Roman authorities tortured Laurence by roasting him on a barbecue grid, but after some time he told them, "I'm cooked on that side, you can turn me over now." The **San Lorenzo River**

[Santa Cruz Co.] was named in 1769, probably for the same saint.

SAN LUCAS [Monterey Co.]. The Spanish name of Saint Luke the Evangelist was applied to a land grant in 1842.

SAN LUIS (LOO is). Spanish for "Saint Louis." **San Luis Obispo,** "Saint Louis the Bishop," was named for the saint who was bishop of Toulouse in the thirteenth century. The mission was founded by Father Serra in 1772; the modern town and **San Luis Obispo County** were founded in 1850. **San Luis Rey** [San Diego Co.], "Saint Louis the King," was named for the saint who was king of France in the thirteenth century; the mission was founded there in 1798. By contrast, **San Luis Creek** [Merced Co.] was named in 1805 not for any Saint Louis, but for Saint Aloysius Gonzaga, an Italian of the sixteenth century.

SAN MARCOS (MAHR kuhs, MAHR kohs) [San Diego Co.]. Named in 1797 for Saint Mark the Evangelist. **San Marcos Pass** [Santa Barbara Co.] was named around 1817, also for the evangelist.

SAN MARINO (muh REE noh) [Los Angeles Co.]. The term was transferred from a place in Maryland, named after the tiny republic surrounded by Italy; this in turn was named for a saintly Italian stonemason and hermit of the fourth century.

SAN MARTIN (mahr TEEN) [Santa Clara Co.]. Named around 1844 by the landowner Martin Murphy, in honor of his patron saint, Saint Martin of Tours, who lived in fourth-century France.

SAN MATEO (muh TAY oh). The name of Saint Matthew, the evangelist and apostle, was applied to **San Mateo Creek** in 1776, and to a settlement in the 1790s. **San**

Mateo County was created in 1856, and the modern town of **San Mateo** in 1863.

SAN MIGUEL (muh GEL) [San Luis Obispo Co.]. Named for the Archangel Michael when the mission was founded in 1797. **San Miguel Island** [Channel Islands, Santa Barbara Co.] was named around 1790. The name has often been pronounced in English as *muh GIL,* as if referring to a "St. McGill."

SAN NICOLAS (NIK uh luhs) ISLAND [Ventura Co.]. Named in 1602 for Saint Nicholas of Myra, the prototype of Santa Claus.

SAN ONOFRE (uh NOH free) [San Diego Co.]. Named for Saint Onuphrius, an Egyptian, around 1828.

SAN PABLO (PAB loh) [Contra Costa Co.]. Refers to Saint Peter the Apostle. **Point San Pablo** was named around 1811, and the name was given to a land grant in 1823.

SAN PASCUAL (pas KWAHL) [San Diego Co.]. Named for Saint Pascal Baylon, a Spaniard of the sixteenth century.

SAN PEDRO (PEE droh, PAY droh) [Los Angeles Co.]. Refers to Saint Peter the Apostle. The name was given to **San Pedro Bay** in 1542, to a land grant in 1784, and to the modern town in 1854. It is now part of the city of Los Angeles.

SAN QUENTIN [KWEN tin, KWIN tin] [Marin Co.]. Refers to a Roman officer of the third century who resigned his commission to become a Christian; he was tortured and beheaded while preaching the gospel in France. However, **San Quentin Point** was first called Punta de Quintín, after an Indian rebel named Quintín who was captured there in 1824. The *San* was added by U.S. authorities in 1850.

SAN RAFAEL (ruh FEL) [Marin Co.]. Refers to the Archangel Raphael. The mission was founded in 1817, and the city around 1841.

SAN RAMON (ruh MOHN) [Contra Costa Co.]. Originally simply Ramón, named before 1833 after a local sheepherder. The *San* was added later, and the modern town came into existence in the 1850s.

SAN REMO (RAY moh) [Monterey Co.]. Named in the late nineteenth century, probably after the town of San Remo on the Italian Riviera. The Italian name was originally based on the name of San Romulo, a fifth-century bishop of Genoa—presumably from the association with Romulus and Remus, founders of Rome.

SAN ROQUE (ROH kay) **CREEK** [Santa Barbara Co.]. Named around 1824 after Saint Roch, a French priest of the fourteenth century.

SAN SIMEON (SIM ee uhn) [San Luis Obispo Co.]. Named around 1819 after Saint Simeon of Jerusalem, a cousin of Jesus. He is said to have been crucified at the age of 120.

SANTA ANA (AN uh) [Orange Co.]. Refers to Saint Anne, the mother of the Virgin Mary. The **Santa Ana River** was named in 1769, but the modern town was not named until 1869. **Santa Anita** (uh NEE tuh) [Los Angeles Co.] refers not to "Saint Annie," but to "little Santa Ana." The name was given to a land grant in 1841.

SANTA BARBARA (BAR bruh). The name refers to a Roman maiden of the third century who was beheaded by her father because she had become a Christian. **Santa Barbara Channel** was named in 1602, the presidio in

1782, and the mission in 1786; the modern city and **Santa Barbara County** were created in 1850.

SANTA CATALINA (kat uh LEE nuh) **ISLAND** [Los Angeles Co.]. Named in 1602 after Saint Catherine, the royal virgin and martyr of Alexandria. According to legend, she was the most beautiful and learned woman of her day; after she had converted many members of the Roman emperor's court to Christianity, the enraged monarch had her executed on a revolving wheel studded with sharp blades. (The usual Spanish form of the name Catherine is Catalina; a rarer variant is Catarina.)

SANTA CLARA (KLAIR uh). Refers to Saint Clare of Assisi, a Franciscan saint of the thirteenth century. In northern California, **Santa Clara Mission** was founded in 1777; **Santa Clara County** was named in 1850. In southern California, the **Santa Clara River** [Los Angeles, Ventura Cos.] was so named in 1769. The **Santa Clarita** (kluh REE tuh) **River** is the "little Saint Clare," so named as a tributary of the Santa Clara.

SANTA CRUZ (KROOZ). Spanish for "holy cross." On Monterey Bay, the name was given to a stream in 1769, and to **Santa Cruz Mission** in 1791. A Spanish settlement called Branciforte, in honor of the viceroy of Mexico, was founded in 1797; the modern town was named Santa Cruz in 1849. **Santa Cruz County** was established in 1850 and first named Branciforte, but renamed Santa Cruz in the same year.

SANTA FE (FAY) **SPRINGS** [Los Angeles Co.]. The Spanish name, meaning "holy faith," was given in 1886 by the Santa Fe Railroad. The rail company was named after the city of Santa Fe, New Mexico, which itself was originally called La Villa Real de la Santa Fe de San Francisco de

Asís, "the royal town of the holy faith of Saint Francis of Assisi."

SANTA LUCIA (loo SEE uh) **RANGE** [San Luis Obispo, Monterey Cos.]. Named in 1602 for the martyred Saint Lucy of Syracuse.

SANTA MARGARITA (mahr guh REE tuh) [San Luis Obispo Co.]. Mentioned in records of 1776; it was probably named for Saint Margaret of Cortona, an Italian saint of the thirteenth century. The **Santa Margarita River** [San Diego Co.] was named in 1769 for Saint Margaret of Antioch, a martyr of the third century.

SANTA MARIA (muh REE uh) [Santa Barbara Co.]. Represents Spanish *Santa María,* "Saint Mary." The name is recorded for a land grant in 1837, and for the **Santa Maria River** in 1850. Here and in other California place names, the term generally refers not to the Virgin, who was usually called Nuestra Señora, "Our Lady," but rather to one of the many other saints named Mary. The Santa Maria River, contrary to usual naming practice, has a different name above its confluence with the Sisquoc River, its principal tributary; it is then called the Cuyama River.

SANTA MONICA (MAHN uh kuh) [Los Angeles Co.]. Refers to Saint Monica, the mother of Saint Augustine; the **Santa Monica Mountains** may have been named in 1770. The name occurs in land grants of 1839, and the town was founded in 1875.

SANTA NELLA (NEL uh) [Merced Co.]. There is no "Saint Nella"; the name probably comes from the Centinela Adobe (from Spanish *sentinela,* "sentinel").

SANTA PAULA (PAW luh) [Ventura Co.]. Probably named for Saint Paula, a Roman matron of the fourth century. The name is recorded in 1834; the modern town was founded in 1872.

SANTA RITA (REE tuh) [Monterey Co.]. Named for Saint Rita of Cascia, who lived in Italy in the fourteenth and fifteenth centuries. The name occurs in a land grant of 1837. **Santa Rita** [Alameda Co.] takes its name from a land grant of 1839.

SANTA ROSA (ROH zuh). Spanish for "Saint Rose". In place names, the reference is usually to Saint Rose of Lima, the first female saint of the Americas, who lived in the sixteenth and seventeenth centuries; but some may refer to Saint Rose of Viterbo, an Italian of the thirteenth century. **Santa Rosa Creek** [Sonoma Co.] was supposedly named in Spanish times by a priest who baptized an Indian girl there with the name of Saint Rose; the city of **Santa Rosa** was named in 1853. **Santa Rosa Island** [Channel Islands, Santa Barbara Co.] was so named by a Spanish expedition in 1602.

SANTA SUSANA (soo ZAN uh) [Ventura Co.]. Named for Saint Susanna, a Roman virgin and martyr of the third century; the term is recorded from 1804.

SANTA VENETIA (vuh NEE shuh) [Marin Co.]. There is no "Saint Venice"; the real-estate development, intended to resemble Venice, Italy, was named in 1914.

SANTA YNEZ (ee NEZ). Refers to Saint Agnes (modern Spanish Inés), a virgin martyr of the early church; **Santa Ynez Mission** [Santa Barbara Co.] was founded in 1804. The **Santa Ynez River** was once called the Purisima but has borne its present name since 1865.

SANTA YSABEL (IZ uh bel) [San Diego Co.]. Named for Saint Elizabeth of Portugal, of the thirteenth and fourteen centuries (modern Spanish is Isabel); the place name is recorded since 1818.

SANTEE (san TEE) [San Diego Co.]. Named for Milton Santee, the first postmaster, in 1892.

SANTIAGO (san tee AH goh) **PEAK** [Orange Co.]. The Spanish name refers to Saint James the Apostle (from Latin *Sanctus Jacobus*). **Santiago Creek** was named in 1769, and the name has been given to the peak since 1894.

SAN TIMOTEO (tim uh TAY oh) **CANYON** [Riverside, San Bernardino Cos.]. So named since 1830, probably in honor of Saint Timothy, a disciple of Saint Paul.

SAN VICENTE (vuh SEN tee) **MOUNTAIN** [Los Angeles Co.]. Refers to one of several holy men called Saint Vincent; the name is recorded since 1802.

SAN YSIDRO (i SEE droh) [San Diego Co.]. The modern Spanish spelling is Isidro; the name probably honors the twelfth-century Spanish saint Isidore the Plowman. The term has been used since 1836.

SAPAGUE (suh PAH way) **CREEK** [Monterey Co.]. Apparently a Rumsen Costanoan name, perhaps from *shapewesh,* "to put out fire."

SARANAP (SAIR uh nap) [Contra Costa Co.]. Coined in 1913 from Sara Naphthaly, the name of the mother of Samuel Naphthaly, vice president of the Oakland and Antioch Railway.

SARATOGA [Santa Clara Co.]. Named in 1867 after Saratoga, New York; the term comes from Mohawk (Iroquoian) *sharató:ken,* meaning "where you get a blister on your heel."

SATICOY (SAT uh koy) [Ventura Co.]. Represents the name of a Chumash Indian village; its meaning is not known.

SAUGUS (SAW gus) [Los Angeles Co.]. Named in 1878 after a town in Massachusetts. The term is an Algonquian word for "outlet."

SAUSALITO (saw suh LEE toh) [Marin Co.]. Named around 1826 to mean "little willow grove." The standard Spanish spelling would be *sauzalito,* from *sauzal,* "willow grove," from *sauz,* "willow."

SCHEELITE (SHEE lite) [Inyo Co.]. Named for the mineral scheelite, an ore of tungsten, which in turn was named for the German chemist Karl W. Scheele.

SCHONCHIN (SKON shin) **BUTTE** [Lava Beds N.M.]. Commemorates the Modoc chief who signed a treaty with the U.S. government in 1864.

SCOTIA (SKOH shuh) [Humboldt Co.]. The company town devoted to the logging industry was named in 1888 after the province of Nova Scotia in Canada; *Scotia* is the Latin word for Scotland.

SCOTTYS CASTLE [Death Valley N.P.]. Built by Walter Scott (alias "Death Valley Scotty"), starting in 1923.

SEAL BEACH [Orange Co.]. Named around 1915 after the marine mammal more accurately called the sea lion.

SEBASTOPOL (suh BAS tuh pohl) [Sonoma Co.]. Named in or soon after 1854, when the siege of the Russian seaport of Sebastopol by the British and French during the Crimean War was in the news.

SECOND GARROTE (guh ROH tee) [Tuolumne Co.]. The Spanish term *garrote* refers to the execution of a criminal by strangulation, or to the scaffold on which the punishment is inflicted. The name Garrote was given in 1850 to the town now called Groveland because a thief was executed there. A similar incident in a camp two miles away led to its being called Second Garrote.

SEIAD (SIE ad) [Siskiyou Co.]. Probably from a Shasta Indian village name; the term is recorded from 1863.

SEIGLER (SEEG luhr) **SPRINGS** [Lake Co.]. Named in the 1870s, with a different spelling, for the original owner, Thomas Sigler.

SEPULVEDA (suh PUHL vuh duh) [Los Angeles Co.]. Named in 1873 for the family of Fernando Sepúlveda, an early settler. A major boulevard in Los Angeles County also bears the name.

SEQUOIA (suh KWOY uh) **NATIONAL PARK** [Tulare Co.]. Named for the giant redwood, classified in 1847 in the genus *Sequoia* (it is currently labeled *Sequoiadendron giganteum*.) The term was intended to honor the Cherokee Indian who invented a writing system for his language.

SERRANO (suh RAH noh). Refers to an Indian tribe living in Riverside and San Bernardino Counties and their language, which belongs to the Takic branch of the Uto-Aztecan family. The term is Spanish for "mountaineer" (from *sierra*).

SESPE (SES pee) [Ventura Co.]. The name of a Chumash village, probably meaning "kneecap."

SHASTA (SHAS tuh). Refers to an Indian tribe and their language, once spoken in Siskiyou County and in an adjacent area of Oregon; the language is now extinct. The term was recorded in 1814 as Shatasla; in 1827, the name was recorded as Sastise and was applied to what we now call **Mount Shasta**. The modern spelling became standard when **Shasta County** was created in 1850.

SHASTINA (shas TEE nuh) [Siskiyou Co.]. This diminutive form of the name Shasta is applied to the west peak of Mount Shasta.

SHOSHONE (shoh SHOH nee). Refers to an Indian tribe, belonging to the Numic branch of the Uto-Aztecan family, living mainly in Nevada, Utah, and Wyoming. The place name in Inyo County was applied to a railroad station shortly after 1900.

SIERRA (see AIR uh). Spanish for "saw blade," and by extension for a mountain range. The term **Sierra Nevada,** "snowy range," was applied to several mountainous areas before it was first given its present usage in 1776. **Sierra County** was named after the range in 1852, and **Sierraville** was established in 1867. **Sierra Madre** (MAH dray) [Los Angeles Co.] refers to the "mother range" of southern California; the town at the foot of the range was so named in 1881.

SIGNAL HILL [Los Angeles Co.]. Named in 1889–90 when a surveyor set up a signal on the hilltop.

SILICON VALLEY [Santa Clara, San Mateo Cos.]. An area in the environs of San Jose that is home to many businesses in the computer industry. The name derives from the silicon chips used in semiconductors for computers.

SILVERADO (sil vuh RAH doh) [Orange Co.]. The name was coined in the 1870s, in analogy to Eldorado, but suggesting silver instead of gold. Another Silverado in Napa County, now vanished, was made famous in Robert Louis Stevenson's *The Silverado Squatters.*

SIMI (suh MEE, SEE mee) [Ventura Co.]. The name of a Ventureño Chumash village.

SINKYONE (SIN kee ohn). Refers to a tribe and language of the Athabaskan family; the language was formerly spoken in coastal Humboldt County. The term is derived from the name applied to these people by the related Kato tribe: *sin-kiyahan,* "coast tribe." It has been used to name **Sinkyone Wilderness State Park**, an area for the preservation of native wildlife and native cultures.

SISAR (si SAHR) **CREEK** [Ventura Co.]. Derived from the name of a Chumash village, *sisá*.

SISKIYOU. The term was Chinook Jargon for "bobtailed horse," apparently borrowed from Cree (Algonquian) *kîskâyowêw,* "bobtailed." It was applied in 1828 by trappers of the Hudson's Bay Company to the **Siskiyou** (SIS kee yoo) **Mountains,** in what is now the border area between Oregon and California. **Siskiyou County** was named in 1852.

SISQUOC (sis KWAHK) [Santa Barbara Co.]. The name is Chumash and means "quail," according to local tradition.

SKY LONDA [San Mateo Co.]. Formerly Sky L'Onda, it was named by a realtor in the 1920s, from the intersection of Skyline Boulevard and La Honda Road.

SMITH RIVER [Del Norte Co.]. Named for the explorer Jedediah Smith, who traveled through this area in 1828. The name Smith River was first applied to what is now the lower Klamath River; it was first attached to the present Smith River in 1851.

SNIKTAW (SNIK taw) **CREEK** [Siskiyou Co.]. Represents the name of a settler called Watkins, spelled backwards.

SOBOBA (suh BOH buh) [Riverside Co.]. The name of a Gabrielino or Luiseño Indian village; it probably is derived from Luiseño *şuvóo-wut,* "winter."

SOCTISH (SAHK tish) **CREEK** [Humboldt Co.]. The local Socktish family, of the Hupa tribe, took their name (with an alternative spelling) from the creek; they believed that the word was from Hupa *sawhjich,* "I put (seeds, granular substance) into my mouth."

SOLANO (suh LAH noh) **COUNTY.** The name was given in 1850, in honor both of Saint Francis Solanus, who preached Christianity in South America in the sixteenth century, and of a local Patwin Indian chief who had been named after the saint. The mission originally named San Francisco Solano [Sonoma Co.] is now usually called Sonoma Mission.

SOLEDAD (SAH luh dad) [Monterey Co.]. The term is Spanish for "solitude"; it was often applied to place names in honor of Nuestra Señora de la Soledad, "Our Lady of Solitude," referring to the loneliness of the Virgin Mary after the Crucifixion. However, the place in Monterey County was supposedly named, in 1776, because the Spaniards asked a local Indian his name, and his answer sounded to them like *Soledad.* When the mission was founded in 1791, it was called La Misión de Nuestra Señora de la Soledad.

SOLIMAR (SOH luh mahr) [Ventura Co.]. Named in the 1920s from Spanish *sol y mar,* "sun and sea."

SOLROMAR (sohl roh MAR) [Ventura Co.]. Coined in the nineteenth century from the Spanish words *sol, oro,* and *mar,* suggesting a "golden sunset on the sea."

SOLVANG (SAHL vang) [Santa Barbara Co.]. Founded by Danes in 1911; the name is Danish for "sun meadow."

SOMIS (SOH muhs) [Ventura Co.]. A Chumash village name; the original meaning is unknown.

SONOMA (suh NOH muh). Derived from a Patwin word for "nose"; an Indian tribe of the area was called Sonomas in Spanish records of 1815. **Sonoma Mission**, as it is now called, was established in 1824 and named San Francisco Solano. The town of Sonoma was founded in 1835, and **Sonoma County** in 1850.

SONORA (suh NOR uh) [Tuolumne Co.]. Established in 1848 by miners from the Mexican state of Sonora.

SOQUEL (soh KEL) [Santa Cruz Co.]. The name of a Costanoan village; the original meaning of the name is unknown.

SOULAJOULE (soo luh HOO lee) **RESERVOIR** [Marin Co.]. Built in 1979 and given the name of a rancho established in 1844, probably derived from Coast Miwok *sówlas,* "laurel," and *húyye,* "promontory."

SQUASH ANN CREEK [Humboldt Co.]. A corruption of Yurok *kwosan,* of unknown meaning.

SQUAW VALLEY [Placer Co.]. The term *squaw* in the name of this winter-sports resort area reflects a widespread word for "woman" in the Algonquian Indian languages; it was first borrowed into English from Massachusett *squà* in 1622. It has been used in many U.S. place names but is now often considered offensive by Native Americans.

STANISLAUS (STAN uh slaw, STAN uh slaws). In 1827–28, an Indian baptized Estanislao, with the name of the Polish saint Stanislaus, ran away from Mission San Jose and became the leader of a rebellious band in the San Joaquin Valley. After the rebels had successfully carried out many raids on Spanish holdings, they were finally defeated by Spanish troops in 1829, on the stream that came to be called the **Stanislaus River**. In 1854 **Stanislaus County** was created.

STARR KING, MOUNT [Yosemite N.P.]. Named during the Civil War for Thomas Starr King, a Unitarian minister of San Francisco, who was influential in keeping California in the Union.

STOCKTON [San Joaquin Co.]. Named for Commodore Robert F. Stockton in 1846, shortly after he had taken possession of California for the United States.

STOVEPIPE WELLS [Death Valley N.P.]. Two springs of good water here were once protected by stovepipes.

SUEY (soo AY) **CREEK** [Santa Barbara Co.]. The Chumash place name is thought to refer to tarweed.

SUGARLOAF [San Bernardino Co.]. In former times, sugar was not sold in bags or boxes, but was delivered in the form of a conical "loaf" to grocers, who would break off pieces and sell it by weight. The term was applied to many hills and mountains in the United States and throughout the world, as witness the Sugarloaf that over-looks Rio de Janeiro.

SUISUN (suh SOON) **BAY** [Contra Costa, Solano Cos.]. Named in 1811 after the Indians of the area, called the Suisunes. The name is Patwin, of unknown origin. **Suisun City** [Solano Co.] takes its name from the bay.

SUNOL (suh NOHL) [Alameda Co.]. Named for Antonio Suñol, a Spaniard in the French navy, who in 1818 jumped ship in Monterey and eventually settled on an Alameda County rancho.

SUR (SER, SOOR), **POINT**, and **SUR RIVER** [Monterey Co.]. The name El Sur, "The South" (i.e., the area south of Monterey), was applied here in 1834. The **Big Sur** and **Little Sur Rivers** are also named for this area.

SUSANVILLE [Lassen Co.]. Named by the pioneer Isaac Roop for his daughter Susan in 1857.

SUSCOL (SUHS kuhl) **CREEK** [Napa Co.]. From the name of a Patwin Indian village; recorded since 1835.

SUTIL (soo TIL) **ISLAND** [Los Angeles Co.]. Named in 1939 after the *Sutil* ("subtle"), a ship in the Spanish exploring expedition of 1792.

SUTRO (SOO troh), **MOUNT** [San Francisco Co.]. Named for Adolph Sutro, a native of Germany, who was mayor of San Francisco from 1894 to 1898.

SUTTER. The pioneer John A. Sutter, born in Germany of Swiss descent, owned a sawmill in the Sacramento Valley at which the Gold Rush began in 1848. He eventually died in poverty, though his name has been given to several California locations. **Sutters Fort** [Sacramento Co.] was founded by him in 1841, as a sort of feudal domain, with Indian serfs whom he trained both as an agricultural work force and as a private militia. The settlement was called Nueva Helvetia, "New Switzerland," and became the terminus of the emigrant trail from Missouri. **Sutter Creek** [Amador Co.] has been so called since Sutter operated a mining camp there in 1849. **Sutter County** was created and named in 1850. **Sutter Buttes** [Sutter Co.] have gone by various names and were often called Marysville Buttes until the name Sutter Buttes was made official in 1949.

SYCAMORE (SIK uh mor) **CANYON** [Ventura Co.]. The area is named for the native sycamore, or plane, tree. Big and Little Sycamore Canyons are named for the size of the trees, not the canyons, since Little Sycamore Canyon is the larger.

SYCUAN (suh KWAHN) **CREEK** [San Diego Co.]. The Diegueño Indian name is said to be from *sekwan,* a kind of bush.

SYLMAR (SIL mahr) [Los Angeles Co.]. Supposed to mean "sea of trees," from Latin *silva,* "forest," plus Spanish *mar,* "sea," referring to the large olive groves that were once here.

TABASECA (tah buh SAY kuh) **TANK** [Riverside Co.]. The name of the desert water hole is from Cahuilla *távish héki',* "home of the red-shafted flicker."

TABOOSE (tuh BOOS) **CREEK** [Inyo Co.]. From the Owens Valley Paiute word for an edible groundnut.

TAFT [Kern Co.]. Named in 1909 for the newly elected president, William Howard Taft.

TAHOE (TAH hoh), **LAKE** [El Dorado, Placer Cos.]. The name is from Washo *dá'aw,* "lake." In 1848, Frémont named it Lake Bonpland in honor of a French botanist; but in 1854 it was renamed Lake Bigler, in honor of John Bigler, governor of California. During the Civil War, when Bigler was known to sympathize with the Confederacy, Union sympathizers started a move to use the name Lake Tahoe, which appeared on a map in 1862. Both names were in use until 1945, when the name Lake Tahoe was made official. The lake has given its name to communities such as **Tahoe City** and **Tahoe Pines.**

TAHQUITZ (TAH kwits, TAH keets, tuh KEETS) **PEAK** [Riverside Co.]. The name is that of a supernatural being, called in Luiseño *táakwish,* in Cahuilla *tákush,* seen in mountainous areas as a fireball.

TAJIGUAS (tuh HIG wuhs, tuh HEE wuhs) [Santa Barbara Co.]. A Chumash village name, perhaps from *tayiyas,* the islay or holly-leafed cherry bush.

TALAWA (TAH luh wuh), **LAKE** [Del Norte Co.]. The term is from Yurok *tolowel,* applied to the Athabaskan tribe living in the area; their name is also spelled Tolowa.

TALLAC (tuh LAK), **MOUNT** [El Dorado Co.]. The term is from Washo *dalá'ak,* "mountain."

TAMALPAIS (tam uhl PIE uhs), **MOUNT** [Marin Co.]. From Coast Miwok *tamal páyiṣ*, literally, "coast mountain"; *tamal* means "west, west coast." The name has nothing to do with Spanish *país*, "land," or with the Mexican food tamales, or even less with tamale pies. The term has been in use in Spanish and English since 1842.

TAMARACK. The true tamarack (eastern larch) is not native to California, but the term is sometimes applied to the lodgepole pine. **Tamarack Peak** [Fresno Co.] and other places are named after this tree.

TANFORAN (tan fuh RAN, TAN fuh ran) [San Mateo Co.]. Named for Toribio Tanfarán, a local farmer in the 1850s; a well-known horse-racing track was built here in the 1920s.

TAPIA (tuh PEE uh) **CANYON** [Los Angeles Co.]. Probably named for the Tapia family, living in this area before 1800.

TARZANA (tahr ZAN uh) [Los Angeles Co.]. Named in 1917 by Edgar Rice Burroughs, the author who created the famous fictional character Tarzan.

TASSAJARA (tas uh HAIR uh) **CREEK** [Monterey Co.]. Represents Spanish *tasajero*, a place where meat is cut in strips and hung in the sun to cure. The area is currently known for its Zen monastery and retreat center.

TEA BAR [Siskiyou Co.]. The name of the Karuk village here was *tíih;* the term *bar* refers in local English to flat land along a river bank.

TECATE (tuh KAH tee) [San Diego Co.]. The site was a Diegueño village; the name may be derived from *tuukatt,* "to cut with an ax," referring to a place where a tree was felled. The term now applies to settlements on both the

U.S. and Mexican sides of the border. The Mexican town contains a large brewery where Tecate Beer is produced.

TECOLOTE (tek uh LOH tee) **VALLEY** [San Diego Co.]. The Mexican Spanish word for "owl" is from Aztec *te-colotl.* There is a **Tecolotito** (tek uh loh TEE toh), or "little owl," **Creek** in Santa Barbara County.

TECOPA (tuh KOH puh) [Inyo Co.]. Named before 1892 after a Southern Paiute elder, *tuku-pïda,* "wildcat arm."

TECTAH (TEK tah) **CREEK** [Humboldt Co.]. From the Yurok village name *tektoh,* meaning "log."

TECUYA (tuh KOO yuh) **CREEK** [Kern Co.]. Said to be the name applied by the Yokuts to the Chumash Indians who occupied the region; the origin is probably Yokuts *thoxil,* "west."

TEHACHAPI (tuh HACH uh pee) [Kern Co.]. From Kawaiisu *tïhachïpía,* supposedly meaning something like "hard climbing." Tehachapi Pass is the site of a major engineering feat of the Southern Pacific Railroad, accomplished in 1876 in such a way that the caboose of a freight train can be directly above its engine in a tunnel below.

TEHAMA (tuh HAY muh). Originally the name of a Wintun village; the meaning is not known. The town was named in 1850, and **Tehama County** in 1856.

TEHIPITE (tuh HIP uh tee) [Kings Canyon N.P.]. May be derived from a Mono term meaning "high rock."

TEJON (tuh HOHN) **CANYON** [Kern Co.]. The Spanish word *tejón* means "badger"; the name was applied here in 1806.

TELEGRAPH HILL [San Francisco Co.]. In 1846, a sailor put up a signal pole here and "telegraphed," as the first message, that a British ship had entered the harbor.

TEMBLOR (tem BLOR) **RANGE** [Kern, San Luis Obispo Cos.]. The Spanish term means "earthquake"; quakes are common in this region.

TEMECULA (tuh MEK yoo luh, tem uh KYOO luh) [Riverside Co.]. A Luiseño Indian village here was recorded as Temeca in 1785, and as Temeco in 1802. The name may be derived from Luiseño *temét,* "sun."

TEMESCAL (tem uh SKAL, TEM uh skal) **LAKE** [Alameda Co.]. This Mexican Spanish word, also spelled *temascal,* means "sweat house," referring to the small house used by Indians for sweating and bathing, comparable to the Finnish sauna. The word is from Aztec *tematlcalli,* containing *tema,* "to bathe," and *calli,* "house." The term survives in place names in several parts of California.

TEMETATE (tem uh TAH tee) **CREEK** [San Luis Obispo Co.]. The name apparently reflects Mexican Spanish *temetate,* a stone slab used for grinding, or its Aztec prototype *temetlatl,* from *tetl,* "stone," and *metlatl,* "grinding slab." However, this is probably a re-formation of the Obispeño Chumash place name *stemeqtatimi,* of unknown meaning.

TENAJA (tuh NAH hah) **CANYON** [Riverside, San Diego Cos.]. From Spanish *tinaja,* " large earthen jar"; the term is often used in the Southwest for a natural water hole.

TENAYA (tuh NIE yuh) **LAKE** [Yosemite N.P.]. The Southern Sierra Miwok name is *ţïyenna,* "sleeping place." Another story, however, is that the lake was named in 1851 by the soldiers who evacuated the Indian population of Yosemite and thought to honor an Indian elder called Ten-ie-ya. As one of the soldiers later wrote, "[the Indian] thought the naming of the lake no equivalent for the loss of his territory."

TENNESSEE COVE [Marin Co.]. Named for the steamer *Tennessee,* wrecked near here in 1853. The ship was named after the state, which was named for the Tennessee River, which in turn was named for a Cherokee town recorded as Tanasqui by the Spanish in 1567.

TEPONA (tuh POH nuh) **POINT** [Humboldt Co.]. From Yurok *tepoona,* derived from *tepoo,* "tree."

TEPO (tuh POH) **RIDGE** [Del Norte Co.]. From a form of Yurok *tepon-,* "to stand, be vertical."

TEPUSQUET (TEP uhs kay) **CREEK** [Santa Barbara Co.]. From Mexican Spanish *tepusque,* a copper coin of low value; it is from Aztec *tepuztli,* "copper." The final *t* was added by a mapmaker's error.

TEQUESQUITE (tek uh SKEE tee) **SLOUGH** [San Benito Co.]. The name is Mexican Spanish for "saltpeter," from Aztec *tequixquitl.*

TERRA BELLA (tair uh BEL uh) [Tulare Co.]. Latin (or Italian) for "beautiful land" (cf. Spanish *tierra bella*), applied here in 1889. **Terra Linda** [Marin Co.], meaning "beautiful land," is said to have been named by Portuguese landowners: hence *terra* instead of Spanish *tierra.*

THERMALITO (ther muh LEE toh) [Butte Co.]. The name is apparently coined from *thermal,* referring to hot springs, plus the Spanish diminutive suffix *-ito.*

THOMES (TAH muhs, TOHMZ) **CREEK** [Tehama Co.]. Named for the landowner Robert H. Thomes.

THOUSAND ISLAND LAKE [Madera Co.]. Belongs to the same class as other California place names like Thousand Palms; but in fact it has around one hundred islets.

TIBURON (TIB uh rahn) [Marin Co.]. From Spanish *tiburón,* "shark"; the name was given to the point in 1823.

TIDOC (TEE dahk) **MOUNTAIN** [Tehama Co.]. From Wintu *t'idooq,* "red ant."

TIERRA. The Spanish word for "land, earth" is repeatedly found in such California place names as **Tierra Buena** (tee AIR uh BWAY nuh) [Sutter Co.], meaning "good earth," and **Tierra del Sol** (del SOHL) [San Diego Co.], "land of the sun." **Tierra Rejada** (ray HAH duh) [Ventura Co.] is local Spanish for "plowed land" (from *reja*, "plow").

TIJERA (tee HAIR uh) [Los Angeles Co.]. The Spanish term means "scissors" or "shortcut," but here it refers to a drainage channel. The name was applied to a land grant in 1823 and is preserved in La Tijera, a Los Angeles branch post office and a street.

TIJUANA (tee WAH nuh) **RIVER** [San Diego Co.]. The name derives from a Diegueño village of unidentifiable origin, but it has often been corrupted to Tía Juana, "Aunt Jane." The city of Tijuana, on the Mexican side of the border, has long been a mecca for tourists from California.

TILTILL CREEK [Yosemite N.P.]. The name is from Southern Sierra Miwok *tiltilna,* "tarweed."

TINEMAHA (TIN uh muh hah), **MOUNT.** The peak was named for a legendary Paiute chief, Tinemaha, brother of Winnedumah.

TIOGA (tie OH guh) **PASS** [Yosemite N.P.]. The name was transferred from Pennsylvania and New York, where it derives from Mohawk (Iroquoian) *teió:ken,* "where it branches in two."

TISH-TANG-A-TANG (tish TANG uh ting [*sic*]) **CREEK** [Humboldt Co.]. From the Hupa village name *diysh-taang'aading,* probably meaning "grouse promontory."

TOCALOMA (toh kuh LOH muh) [Marin Co.]. A Coast Miwok name, perhaps containing *lúme,* "willow."

TOIYABE (toy YAH bee) **NATIONAL FOREST**. Though most of the forest is in Nevada, it extends into Mono and Alpine Counties. The name is from Shoshone *toyapin,* "mountain."

TOKOPAH (TOH kuh pah) **FALLS** [Sequoia N.P.]. The name is said to be Yokuts for "high mountain valley."

TOLOWA (TAH luh wuh). Refers to an Indian tribe and language of the Athabaskan family; the language is spoken in Del Norte County. The term reflects the name of the tribe in the neighboring Yurok language: *tolowel.* With a different spelling, the word occurs in the name of **Talawa Lake**.

TOLUCA (tuh LOO kuh) **LAKE** [Los Angeles Co.]. The name Toluca was originally applied to the settlement of North Hollywood; it was probably a transfer name from the city of Toluca in Mexico, derived from Aztec *tolocan.*

TOMALES (tuh MAH luhs) **BAY** [Marin Co.]. The term refers to the Tamal Indians; their name is from Coast Miwok *támal,* "west, west coast." There is no connection with the Mexican food known as tamales.

TOMKI (TAWM kie) **CREEK** [Mendocino Co.]. From Northern Pomo *miṭhóm kháy,* literally, "splash valley," originally the name of Little Lake Valley.

TOPANGA (tuh PANG guh) [Los Angeles Co.]. A Gabrielino place name, *topa'nga,* of unknown origin.

TOPATOPA (toh puh TOH puh) **MOUNTAINS** [Ventura Co.]. The name refers to a Chumash Indian village near Ojai, perhaps originally *tip tip,* "brushy place."

TOPOCK (TOH pahk) [San Bernardino Co.]. From Mojave *tuupák,* derived from the verb *tapák-,* "to drive piles."

TOPO (TOH poh) **CREEK** [Monterey, San Benito Cos.]. The Spanish word means "mole" elsewhere, but in California it was applied to the gopher.

TORO. The Spanish word for "bull" has been applied to many California places. **Toro** (TOR oh) **Creek** [Monterey Co.] was named in 1834 for a "bobtailed bull." The town of **El Toro** [Orange Co.] was named in 1838.

TORRANCE [Los Angeles Co.]. Named in 1911 for the landowner Jared S. Torrance.

TOYON (TOY ahn). The name of this shrub, also known as California holly or Christmas berry (*Heteromeles arbutifolia*), is used for a number of places, including communities in Calaveras and Shasta Counties. The California Spanish word *toyón* is from Costanoan *totčon*.

TRABUCO (truh BOO koh) **CANYON** [Orange Co.]. The Spanish word for "blunderbuss," an archaic type of gun, was given to the place by soldiers in 1769.

TRACY [San Joaquin Co.]. Named in 1878 for Lathrop J. Tracy, an official of the Southern Pacific Railroad.

TRANCAS (TRANG kuhs) **CREEK** [Los Angeles Co.]. The name is from Spanish *tranca*, "barrier, crossbar."

TRANQUILLON (trang KWIL yuhn) **MOUNTAIN** [Santa Barbara Co.]. The name was applied in 1873; a possible Chumash origin has not been confirmed.

TREASURE ISLAND [San Francisco Co.]. The name was given to the artificial island built by U.S. Army engineers in San Francisco Bay for the 1939–40 world's fair, recalling the title of the famous novel by Robert Louis Stevenson.

TRES PINOS (trays PEE nohs) [San Benito Co.]. Spanish for "three pines." The earlier pronunciation *trays PEE* *nuhs* is now usually avoided because of homophony with *penis*.

TRINIDAD (TRIN uh dad) [Humboldt Co.]. The Spanish term for the (Holy) Trinity was given to the bay by the expedition that entered it in 1775. The town was founded in 1850.

TRINITY. The name was first applied to the **Trinity River** in 1845 by a pioneer who was under the mistaken impression that it emptied into Trinidad Bay. The **Trinity Mountains** were named around 1848, and **Trinity County** in 1850.

TRIUNFO (trie UN foh) **CANYON** [Ventura Co.]. In 1770 Spanish explorers named this area for the Triunfo del Dulcísimo Nombre de Jesús, "Triumph of the sweetest name of Jesus."

TRONA (TROH nuh) [San Bernardino Co.]. Refers to a mineral consisting of sodium carbonate and bicarbonate; it was applied here in 1914.

TRUCKEE (TRUK ee) [Placer, Nevada Cos.]. The name is that of a Northern Paiute leader and supposedly means "all right." The name was applied to the Truckee River in 1844, and to the town in 1864.

TUBA CANYON [Death Valley N.P.]. Not named for the musical instrument, but derived from Panamint *tïpa,* "pine nut."

TUBATULABAL (tuh bah tuh lah BAHL). Refers to a tribe and language of the Uto-Aztecan family, native to Kern County. The term means "pine-nut eaters."

TUCKI (TUK ie, TUK ee) **MOUNTAIN** [Death Valley N.P.]. Called Tucki or Sheep Mountain in 1909. The source may be Shoshone *tukku,* "mountain sheep."

TUEEULALA (too ee LAH luh) **FALLS** [Yosemite N.P.].
Perhaps from Miwok *ti"ele-la*, "shallow place."

TUJUNGA (tuh HUNG guh) [Los Angeles Co.]. The
name of a Gabrielino village; its original meaning is not
known.

TULE (TOO lee). The common California word for the
cattail or bulrush is derived from Mexican Spanish *tule,*
from Aztec *tollin;* the Spanish word *tular* refers to a
place where tules grow, and both terms occur in many
California place names. The *tulares* of the San Joaquin
Valley were noted by the Spanish from 1772 onward.
The name **Tule River** [Tulare Co.] is known from 1850,
and **Tulare** (too LAIR ee, too LAIR) **County** from 1852.
The city of **Tulare** [Kings Co.] was named in 1872. The
disease tularemia was so named because it was first
identified in Tulare County; it has nothing to do with
tulares as such. In northern California, **Tule Lake** [Sis-
kiyou Co.] was named Rhett Lake in 1846 but has
been known by its present name since around 1900. **Tu-
larcitos** (too ler SEE tohs) **Creek** [Monterey Co.] is
named with the Spanish diminutive form, meaning "little tule patches."

TULUCAY (TUL uh kay) **CREEK** [Napa Co.]. Derived
from Patwin *tu'luka*, "red."

TUNA CANYON [Los Angeles Co.]. Does not refer to tuna
fish, but rather is from Spanish *tuna*, the prickly pear; the
word originally comes from the Taino language of the
West Indies. **Tunitas** (too NEE tuhs) **Creek** [San Mateo
Co.] refers to "little prickly pears."

TUNAWEE (TUN uh wee) **CANYON** [Inyo Co.]. From
Panamint *tïnapi*, the bush called "mountain mahog-
any"—pronounced something like *TUN uh vee.*

TUNEMAH (TOO nuh mah) **PASS** [Kings Canyon N.P.]. The name is a Cantonese obscenity, applied by Chinese cooks because of the rough terrain. The original form is *diu nei aa maa*, meaning "Fuck your mother!"

TUNNABORA (too nuh BOR uh) **PEAK** [Sequoia N.P.]. The name is probably from Panamint *tuu*, "black," plus *napatïn*, "canyon."

TUOLUMNE (too AHL uh mee). The name is that of Indians who once lived on the banks of the Stanislaus River; the origin is Central Sierra Miwok *ṭaawalïmni*, "squirrel place," from *ṭaawali*, "squirrel." The **Tuolumne River** has been so named since 1848, and **Tuolumne County** since 1850.

TURLOCK [Stanislaus Co.]. In 1871, the landowner John W. Mitchell modestly declined to have the site named for him; he suggested the present name, after Turlough, Ireland.

TURPENTINOM (ter puhn TIE nuhm) **CREEK** [Shasta Co.]. From Wintu *čur-pantinom,* presumably with folk-etymological influence of English *turpentine.*

TYEE (TIE ee) **LAKES** [Kings Canyon N.P.]. Named in 1936 for Tyee, a brand of salmon eggs used as bait. The word means "chief" in Chinook Jargon, once used as a trade language among Indians and whites in the Pacific Northwest. The term originally comes from the Nootka language of Vancouver Island, British Columbia.

UBEHEBE (yoo bee HEE bee) **CRATER** [Death Valley N.P.]. Local Panamint Indians suggest that the English name is from Owens Valley Paiute *hïbï-bici,* "woman's breasts"—originally applied to the Wahguyhe Peaks.

UKIAH (yoo KIE uh) [Mendocino Co.]. From Central Pomo *yó-qhaaya,* "south valley"; the term entered Spanish as Yokaya around 1845. The present town was named in 1856.

UKONOM (YOO kuh nahm) **CREEK** [Siskiyou Co.]. From the Karuk village *yuhnaam,* probably meaning "down-river flat."

UMUNHUM (YOO muh nuhm), **MOUNT** [Santa Clara Co.]. Perhaps from a Costanoan word for "humming-bird," such as Rumsen *ummun.*

USAL (YOO sawl) [Mendocino Co.]. From Northern Pomo *yoosal,* perhaps containing *yoo,* "south."

USONA (yoo SOH nuh) [Mariposa Co.]. An acronym for United States of North America; the name was applied in 1913.

UVAS (YOO vuhs) **CREEK** [Santa Clara Co.]. From the Spanish word for "grapes," referring to the presence of wild grape vines.

VACAVILLE (VAK uh vil) [Solano Co.]. Named for the Vaca family, who came to California in 1841 from New Mexico, where the Spanish word *vaca,* "cow," is a common surname.

VALLECITO (val uh SEE toh) [San Diego Co.]. Spanish for "little valley" (from *valle,* "valley"); the name dates from 1854.

VALLEJO (vuh LAY hoh, vuh LAY oh) [Solano Co.]. Founded in 1850 by General Mariano G. Vallejo, an important landowner and public figure under both Mexican and American rule; he introduced vineyards and winemaking at his estate in Sonoma County.

VALYERMO (val YAIR moh) [Los Angeles Co.]. A combination of two Spanish elements: *val* for *valle,* "valley," plus *yermo,* "barren."

VAN DUZEN (van DOO zuhn) **RIVER** [Humboldt, Trinity Cos.]. Named by an exploring party in 1850, after one of its members, James Van Duzen.

VAN NUYS (van NIEZ) [Los Angeles Co.]. Named in 1912 for Isaac N. Van Nuys, who grew wheat in the area.

VASQUEZ (vas KWEZ, VAS kuhz) **ROCKS** [Los Angeles Co.]. Named for the bandit Tiburcio Vásquez, who had a hideout in this area. The picturesque rocky scenery has often been used as a site for cowboy movies. The bandit was captured in Los Angeles in 1874 and executed.

VENICE [Los Angeles Co.]. Built in 1904 with a system of canals for thoroughfares, complete with gondoliers, in imitation of Venice, Italy. Some of the canals still exist.

VENTANA (ven TAN uh) **CONE** [Monterey Co.]. The Spanish word for "window" was applied because of a windowlike opening in one of the hills.

VENTURA (ven TOOR uh). The Mission of San Buenaventura was founded in 1782, named after the Italian Saint Bonaventure (literally, "good luck") of the thirteenth century. The river was so named in 1830. A post office with the same name was established in 1861. In 1872 the county was created with the name **Ventura County,** and in 1891 the town was also given the abbreviated name **Ventura.** The **Ventura River** has been commonly so called since 1895.

VERDI (VER die) **PEAK** [Sierra Co.]. Named for the Italian opera composer Giuseppe Verdi.

VERDUGO (ver DOO goh) **CANYON** [Los Angeles Co.]. Named for a family of early settlers; José María Verdugo received a land grant in 1784. The Spanish name has nothing to do with *verde,* "green"; it means "hangman" or "executioner." **Verdugo City** was founded in 1925.

VERNAL FALL [Yosemite N.P.]. The name is from the Latin word for "springtime," because of the cool green surroundings.

VICTORVILLE [San Bernardino Co.]. Named for J. N. Victor, construction superintendent of the California Southern Railroad in 1888–89.

VIEJAS (VEE uhs) **VALLEY** [San Diego Co.]. In 1846 a Spanish expedition supposedly gave the name Valle de las Viejas, "valley of the old women," to an Indian village here because at their approach the inhabitants fled, leaving behind only the old women.

VISALIA (vie SAYL yuh) [Tulare Co.]. Probably named after Visalia, Kentucky, which in turn had been named for a relative of Nathaniel Vise, a founder of the California town.

VISITATION (viz uh TAY shun) **VALLEY** [San Francisco, San Mateo Cos.]. The Spanish name, La Visitación, refers to the occasion when the Virgin Mary visited her cousin Saint Elizabeth.

VISTA (VIS tuh) [San Diego Co.]. Spanish for "view." The term was occasionally used for naming places in Spanish times, as in the widespread **Buena Vista,** "good view"; but most names that include the word are modern applications—for example, **Vista del Mar** [Los Angeles Co.].

VIZCAINO (vis kah EE noh), **CAPE** [Mendocino Co.]. The Spanish explorer Sebastián Vizcaíno sailed up the California coast in 1602–3.

VOGELSANG (VOH guhl sang) **PEAK** [Yosemite N.P.]. Named in 1907 for Charles A. Vogelsang, of the State

Fish and Game Commission. The German name originally had the meaning "a meadow where birds sing."

VOLCANO [Amador Co.]. Named around 1850; there was never a volcano here, but miners believed that underground caverns might have been evidence of earlier volcanic activity.

WABENA (wah BEE nuh) **CREEK** [Placer Co.]. Named for the pioneer Wabena or Wubbena family, originally from the Netherlands.

WAHGUYHE (WAH gie) **PEAKS** [Death Valley N.P.]. The term may be from Panamint *waa-kko'e,* "pinyon-pine summit."

WAHTOKE (WAH tohk) [Fresno Co.]. Probably from Yokuts *watak,* "pine nut."

WAITISAW (WAY tuh saw) [Shasta Co.]. From Wintu *wayti sawal,* "north pond."

WALTERIA (wahl TAIR ee uh) [Los Angeles Co.]. For a Captain Walters, who built a hotel here early in the twentieth century.

WAPAMA (wuh PAH muh) **FALLS** [Tuolumne Co.]. Perhaps from Sierra Miwok *wepaama,* from *weepa,* "uphill."

WAPPO (WAH poh). Refers to an Indian tribe and language, of the Yukian family, native to Napa and Sonoma Counties. The term was applied by whites, based on Spanish *guapo,* "handsome, brave."

WASCO (WAHS koh) [Kern Co.]. Named by the pioneer William Bonham after his home in Wasco County, Oregon; that area had been named for a Chinookan Indian tribe.

WASHO (WAH shoh). Refers to an Indian tribe and language of Alpine County and of adjacent Washoe County, Nevada; the term is from *wáašiw,* the tribe's name for themselves. **Washoe Creek** [Sonoma Co.] was probably named for the Washoe Mine, the name having been transferred from Nevada.

WASSUMA (wah SOO muh) **CREEK** [Madera Co.]. Refers to a Southern Sierra Miwok village. It may be related to *wasaama,* the location of an Indian ceremonial house at Ahwanee, perhaps containing *wassa,* "ponderosa pine."

WAUCOBA (wuh KOH buh) **MOUNTAIN** [Inyo Co.]. From Owens Valley Paiute *wokóbï* or Northern Paiute *wogópi,* "bull pine"; the English name is used locally for various pine species.

WAWONA (wah WOH nuh) [Yosemite N.P.]. From Southern Sierra Miwok *wohwohna,* "redwood tree," supposedly imitating the hoot of the owl, with which the trees were mythically linked. It is said that Indians considered the trees sacred and believed that anyone who cut them would be visited with bad luck by the owl.

WEAVERVILLE [Trinity Co.]. Named for George Weaver, a prospector, who built the first cabin in 1850.

WEED [Siskiyou Co.]. Named in 1900 for the lumberman Abner Weed, a native of Maine.

WEIMAR (WEE mahr) [Placer Co.]. Named in 1886 in memory of "old Weimah," a local Indian elder. The spelling was assimilated to that of the city in Germany.

WEITCHPEC (WICH pek) [Humboldt Co.]. From Yurok *wecpek* or *wecpus,* "confluence," referring to the place where the Trinity River flows into the Klamath River.

WEOTT. *See* Wiyot.

WHITNEY, MOUNT [Tulare, Inyo Cos.]. Named in 1864 for geologist Josiah Dwight Whitney.

WHITTIER [Los Angeles Co.]. Founded in 1887 by an organization of Quakers, and named in honor of the Quaker poet John Greenleaf Whittier.

WILDOMAR (WIL duh mahr) [Riverside Co.]. Named in 1883 by combining the given names of the founders: William Collier, Donald Graham, and Margaret Collier Graham.

WILLITS [Mendocino Co.]. Named in the late 1870s for the pioneer Hiram Willits.

WILLOWS [Glenn Co.]. Named in 1876 for a pond on the site, surrounded by willow trees.

WILMINGTON [Los Angeles Co.]. Named in 1863 by the founder, Phineas Banning, after his birthplace in Delaware.

WILSON, MOUNT [Los Angeles Co.]. Named in 1864 for Benjamin D. ("Don Benito") Wilson, who built a burro trail up the mountain. He was the first mayor of Los Angeles under U.S. rule.

WINNEDUMAH (win uh DOO muh) [Inyo Co.]. This granite monolith is named for a Paiute medicine man, who according to legend turned into rock during a battle with an enemy tribe.

WINNETKA (wuh NET kuh) [Los Angeles Co.]. Named in 1947 after Winnetka, Illinois; that name is said to have been coined by whites on the basis of Algonquian *winne,* "beautiful."

WINNIBULLI (WIN uh bul ee) [Shasta Co.]. From Wintu *wenem buli,* "middle mountain."

WINTUN (WIN toon). A cover term for three related tribes and languages of the Sacramento Valley: Wintu in

Trinity and Shasta Counties, Nomlaki in Tehama County, and Patwin in Glenn and Colusa Counties. The term is derived from *winthuun,* meaning "human being" in the Wintu language. It forms part of the name of **Wintun Glacier** in Siskiyou County.

WITTAWAKET (WIE tuh wah kuht) **CREEK** [Shasta Co.]. From Wintu *witee waqat,* "turn creek."

WIYOT (WEE yaht). Refers to a tribe and to its language, related to the Algonquian languages of the eastern United States. The language was once spoken in Humboldt County but is now extinct. In 1860 much of the tribe was destroyed by whites in a great massacre at Eureka. The term is from *wíyo't,* the Wiyot name for the Eel River. The spelling **Weott** is used for a settlement established in 1926.

WYANDOTTE (WIE uhn daht) [Butte Co.]. Named for a party of Wyandot (Iroquoian) Indians from Kansas who prospected in the vicinity in 1850. The tribe's name in their own language is *wendat.*

XIMENO (hi MAY noh) [Los Angeles Co.]. Represents an old-fashioned spelling of the Spanish name Jimeno. The term may preserve the memory of Manuel Jimeno Casarín.

YAHI (YAH hee). Refers to an Indian tribe and language of the Yana language family; the language was once spoken in Tehama County. This was the language of Ishi, who became famous in 1911 as the last "wild Indian" in California. The name is preserved at the site of **Yahi Indian Camp.**

YANA (YAH nuh). Refers to a family of Indian languages once spoken in Shasta and Tehama Counties; the term is based on the native word for "human being."

YANG-NA. A Spanish spelling for the name of the Gabrielino village on the site of which the city of Los Angeles was founded. The Indian name is more accurately *iyáanga',* "poison-oak place."

YCATAPOM (wie KAH tuh pohm, wye KAT uh pohm) **PEAK** [Shasta, Trinity Cos.]. The name is from Wintu *wayk'odipom,* "north step place."

YDALPOM (wie DAL pahm) [Shasta Co.]. From Wintu *waydalpom,* "place to the north."

YERBA BUENA (yer buh BWAY nuh) **ISLAND** [San Francisco Bay]. Preserves the name of Yerba Buena Cove, an early area of settlement in what is now the city of San Francisco. The Spanish term, meaning "good herb," refers to a native plant resembling mint, with a sweet scent.

YERMO (YER moh) [San Bernardino Co.]. Spanish for "barren"; the name was given to this desert site around 1908.

YGNACIO (ig NAH see oh, ig NAY see oh) **VALLEY** [Contra Costa Co.]. The modern Spanish spelling for this name is Ignacio; it probably refers to Ignacio Martínez, after whom the town of Martinez was named.

YOKUTS (YOH kuhts). Refers to a group of related Indian tribes and languages, found in Madera, Fresno, and Tulare Counties. The term is based on the native word for "human being" and is singular, not plural; there is no such thing as a "Yokut Indian."

YOLLA BOLLY (YOH luh boh lee) **MOUNTAINS** [Trinity, Tehama Cos.]. Represents Wintu *yoola buli,* "snow mountain."

YOLO (YOH loh). Originally a Patwin Indian name, of unknown meaning. It was applied to the county in 1850.

YONTOCKETT (YAHN tah kuht) [Del Norte Co.]. From the Tolowa Indian village *yan'-dagɔd,* literally, "southward uphill."

YORBA LINDA (yor buh LIN duh) [Orange Co.]. This term contains the name of the Yorba family, among the earliest Spanish pioneers of California. The combination Yorba Linda was coined around 1913; the element Linda is not the Spanish word for "pretty," but is from the name of nearby Olinda. Yorba Linda was the birthplace of Richard M. Nixon.

YOSEMITE (yoh SEM uh tee) [Mariposa County]. From Southern Sierra Miwok *yohhe'meti* or *yoṣṣe'meti,* "they are killers," evidently a name given to the Indians of the valley by those outside it. A derivation from Southern Sierra Miwok *ihiimaṭi* or *iṣiimaṭi,* "grizzly bear," is not accurate. The name was applied to the valley by whites in 1851.

YOUNTVILLE (YOWNT vil) [Napa Co.]. Named for George C. Yount, a pioneer of 1831.

YREKA (wie REE kuh) [Siskiyou Co.]. The name, given in 1852, is from *wáik'a',* the Shasta Indian name for Mount Shasta. The city contains a business whose name forms a palindrome: Yreka Bakery.

YUBA (YOO buh). Originally the name of a Maidu Indian village, spelled Yubu in early records and applied to the **Yuba River** by 1844. **Yuba City** [Sutter Co.] was laid out and named after the river in August 1849, and **Yuba County** was formed in 1850.

YUCAIPA (yoo KIE puh) [San Bernardino Co.]. The name is recorded in 1841; it is supposedly derived from a Serrano term for "wet or marshy land."

YUCCA (YUK uh) **VALLEY** [San Bernardino Co.]. Named in 1915 for *Yucca brevifolia,* the Joshua tree.

YUHWAMAI (yoo wah MIE) [San Diego Co.]. From Luiseño *yuxwáamay,* "little mud," derived from *yuxwáala,* "mud."

YUKIAN (YOO kee uhn). Refers to a family of related Indian tribes and languages of Mendocino, Sonoma, and Napa Counties; the Yuki, Huchnom, and Wappo belong to this family. All the Yukian languages are now extinct. The term is derived from the name applied by the neighboring Wintu tribe: *yuke,* "enemy."

YUMA (YOO muh). Refers to an Indian tribe living in Imperial County and in the area around the city of Yuma, Arizona, and to their language. However, the tribe and language are now officially called Quechan. The term *Yuma* also survives in the name of the Yuman language family, a grouping that also includes several other Indian languages of California, Arizona, and Mexico.

YUROK (YOO rahk). Refers to an Indian tribe and guage of Humboldt and Del Norte Counties guage is related to the Algonquian languag ern United States. The term is not nati by whites from the word *yúruk* neighboring Karuk language river"). The Yurok are no for "downriver" in thei

ZABRISKIE POINT [Death Valley N.P.]. Named for Christian B. Zabriskie, director of the Pacific Coast Borax Company. The location gave its name to a 1970 film by the Italian director Michelangelo Antonioni.

ZACA (ZAK uh) **LAKE** [Santa Barbara Co.]. Refers to a Chumash Indian village or its chief; the name occurs in an 1838 land grant.

ZAMORA (zuh MOR uh) [Yolo Co.]. So named in 1910. It appears as a place name in Spain and Mexico and is also a Spanish family name.

ZANJA COTA (zahn hah KOH tuh) **CREEK** [Santa Barbara Co.]. The Spanish word *zanja* means "irrigation ditch"; Cota is the name of a local family. The place name dates from 1795.

ZAYANTE (zie AN tee) **CREEK** [Santa Cruz Co.]. Probably from Rumsen (Costanoan) *sayyan-ta,* "at the heel"; Spanish records refer to Sayanta in 1834.

ZINFANDEL (ZIN fan duhl) [Napa Co.]. Named before 1900, after the zinfandel wine grape. The grape probably reflects a Czech grape name, *cinifádl,* derived in turn from a German term such as *Zierfahndler.*

ZZYZX (ZIZ iks, ZIE ziks) [San Bernardino Co.]. The site of a local radio station with the supposed call letters ZZYZX, operated by an eccentric desert dweller.